LONGMAN ENGLISH 2

R B HEATH
T McSWEENEY

GW00370931

Longman

Contents

The short story

Playscript   **Noah** *André Obey*

Poetry

CONTENTS

Thinking things over

Descriptions

A few more difficult

The language we use

*Poems with assignments

☐ This symbol links a question with a picture.

MISCELLANY

1 Information

Contents

Family Life in India

Hari Joshi was born into a high-caste Indian family in January, 1924, the youngest of three brothers. He was a clever boy, but did not continue his studies after taking his O Levels because he wanted to start earning money. In India the ties between the father and his sons, and also between brothers, are very strong. When one brother falls ill or is out of work the other members of the family take on the responsibility of caring for him and his children. Sometimes several brothers and their children live in the same house and become an 'extended' family. Hari's eldest brother was frequently out of

10 work because he had no qualifications. It was to help him and his children that Hari left school and started teaching. His plan was to earn and learn at the same time, so he studied in the early mornings at a special college in order to gain qualifications. In this way he gained a Secondary Teachers' Certificate, a Bachelor of Arts Degree, and a Bachelor of Education Degree. It took him thirteen years of hard work to pass the necessary examinations.

A Hindu marriage ceremony

When Hari was twenty-seven years old some friends of his parents came and suggested that their eighteen-year-old daughter should become Hari's wife. It is usual in India for parents to arrange
20   marriages for their children, but Hari's father consulted him about it. Hari said he would like to see the girl before consenting to the marriage, and a meeting was arranged. When Hari saw Harbala he fell in love with her and thanked God for sending the right girl into his life. He explained to her his responsibilities to his family and she was willing to help him care for them; so they became engaged.

In Western countries an engagement may be a private affair between two people, with the giving of a ring. In India an engagement is a colourful and important occasion at which the betrothed couple make their promises to each other in the presence of their
30   families and friends. So it was with Hari and Harbala.

Three months later they were married. In India all the relatives, friends and sometimes whole villages are invited to weddings. On the first day there were 700 guests at Hari's wedding, and 200 on the second. The ceremony was a long one. It started at 10.30 p.m. and lasted throughout the night. In a Hindu marriage a sacred fire is lit and the couple move several times around the fire, throwing certain scented spices into it. The heart of the ceremony is the promises which the couple make to be faithful to each other throughout their lives. All the vows are taken in the presence of relatives and friends,
40   and most Indian couples remain faithful. Hari and Harbala have had many difficulties to face in their married life, but they have never wavered in their love for each other.

Nora Cook
Modern Stories for School Assembly

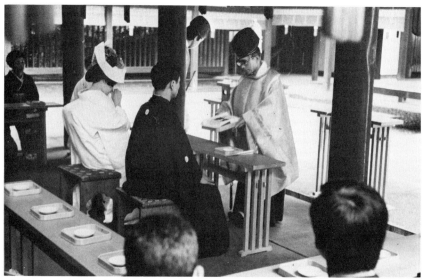

A Japanese marriage ceremony. The white band around the bride's hair is supposed to hide the horns of feminine jealousy.

Summing up

1 What information tells us
  a that Hari had the ability to continue his education?
  b the reason why he did not continue it?
2 Make a list of the examples given of the way members of Indian families help each other.
3 What is the first paragraph mainly about? Two or three words will be sufficient for the answer.

Comprehension and discussion

4 How can you tell from the information and examples given in the first paragraph that the male members of an Indian family were thought to be the most important?
5 What was unusual about Hari's marriage?
6 In what ways were a son's responsibilities to his family different from those of a daughter, e.g. Harbala?
7 Find out what the following words and phrases mean as used in the passage:
  a high caste
  b extended families
  c ties between father and son

Activities and research

8 Find out all you can about the caste system in India; why it was introduced and why it was stopped. Do any other societies have similar systems? How fair do you think they are?
9 Find out and describe how engagement and wedding ceremonies are conducted for people of other nationalities and religions, e.g. Jewish customs, Moslem customs.

Oral ideas

10 Prepare a short talk on the ways that engagements and weddings in Britain differ from those in India.

A newly-married Jewish couple stand under the wedding canopy.

Living in a Village

There are thousands of villages in England and Scotland — and each one has its own particular 'feel' which has nothing to do with physical characteristics. Even so, villagers can usually be divided into three groups: Natives — people who were born here, and have never moved away. Returners — people who were born in the village, left, and came back. Newcomers — people moving in from outside, either to work, to commute, or to retire.

Meet some of them:

ANGUS MACLEAN, 33, manager of the sawmill. Was an estate worker in the Highlands, saw the chance of promotion, and moved in with his family.

'It's all right here, I suppose. But we'll be away back to the mountains in a couple of years. The shooting and fishing just aren't the same!'

RICHARD ELLIS, 17, a native of the village, apprenticed to the blacksmith. Plans to finish his apprenticeship, work for a while, then start up in business on his own.

'The work's there, isn't it? You've only got to look around. And you can get a lot of help too. Setting up in a village.'

GRANT NEWBY, 15, son of the local builder, born in the village, but has to travel to comprehensive school in the nearby town. A Scout and a keen footballer — in the village team. Sometimes goes to the Youth Club.

'I'll be joining my Dad in the business when I leave school. Can't wait! Got to get some qualifications first, though — still I suppose you can see the point.'

DERMOTT BROCK, 43, a newcomer. Used to work for a large Midland ceramics concern, but the pressure became too much. Set up his own one-man craft pottery 7 years ago — now it's thriving, even beginning to export.

'Love it here. Fresh air, fields, village life. Wouldn't get me back in a city — that's for sure.'

SALLY GREEN, 63, the village postmistress, and a native — rarely having been away. Very little happens without her knowing about it. President of the local Women's Institute, and a Church Warden.

'Couldn't imagine living anywhere else — not at all. Here you've got all your family and neighbours and friends around you. I wouldn't change a thing.'

EMILY MEAD, 22, born in the village, she now works as a machinist in the clothing factory. Engaged to a mechanic at the garage. They plan to settle down in part of her widowed father's house.

'I'm really glad I got this job — otherwise I'd have nothing to do but look after Dad. The money's handy too — with us saving up.'

ARCHIE-SWAIN, 55, a village boy, joined the Merchant Navy because there was no work. Married and returned to the village when his father left him some property, now a fish-farm. A parish-councillor and a keen morris-dancer.

'We're part of the scenery again — shan't leave again. This is where my roots are.'

STELLA BRINSCOMBE, 18, moved here with her parents six year ago. Last year's Carnival Queen. Now commutes to nearby town to train as a hairdresser.

'I'm going to have my own salon before I'm 25, but I don't suppose it'll be here. I mean, it's just not big enough for a quality salon, is it? And if I move away, I can't see myself coming back — except for visits.'

HAZEL METCALFE, 19, born in Manchester, but loved the country — so she moved out. Now permanent receptionist at the hotel. As an ex-art student she hopes to start selling sketches through the local craft shop. Most evenings off are spent at the cinema or disco in the nearby market town.

'It's great really — but you do tend to keep seeing the same old faces.'

ROD WILSON, 28, the vet. Son of the vicar, born in the village — but had to go away to college. Returned when the local practice became available. Married with one child.

'If you don't like darts, football or cricket, there's not a lot to do locally — but I've just taken up bell-ringing!'

Comprehension and discussion

1 Group the people described into the three categories.
2 Which of the people do you think will change where they live?
3 Which people have found work in the village?
4 Which people have had to go outside the village for work?
5 Make a list of the recreation activities in the village.
6 How true is it to say that most of the young people want to move away to the towns whereas the village appeals to the older people? Give examples.
7 What do the following have in common and how do they differ?
　a Dermott Brock and Hazel Metcalfe
　b Stella Brinscombe and Angus Maclean
　c Emily Mead and Sally Green
　d Sally Green and Archie Swain

8 From the information given, which of the people described do you think would enjoy living in a town? Give reasons.

Writing

9 What are the advantages and disadvantages of living in a village?
10 How important are the following to people who live in the village?
　Write four to five lines on each.
　a A school
　b Good bus service
　c Car
　d Church
　e Small workplaces
11 Try to describe what you imagine the effect would be on a village if the following happened:
　a a very large firm built a factory near to the village;
　b a main road or motorway was built nearby.

Which Cost More — Sons or Daughters?

There's no price tag attached to children — but all parents would agree that over the years, children cost money. Lots of it!

Some of the cost of bringing up children is hidden in general expenditure like household electricity or the family food bill. Other items are easier to calculate; for example, the price tag on your latest pair of jeans!

But are the costs the same for each family, and, in particular, do boys cost more than girls?

'Payday' asked some parents and children for their views, and it quickly became obvious that few 'teenagers' had ever thought of themselves as a 'cost' before. On the other hand, parents budgeted very carefully for their children. Not surprising really — they're the ones who have to find most of the money! More or less everyone agreed that, up to the age of about 10, it makes little difference financially whether it's a boy or a girl in the family. Clothes, toys, pocket money, comics, sports and hobbies cost about the same. Then things change.

Clothes

'They both become fashion conscious,' said one mother, 'but where there may be racks and racks of dresses for girls, there'll only be a couple of rails of trousers for boys! You can shop around and get girls' clothes cheaper but there aren't the alternatives for boys.'

True or false?

Some boys protested that girls are fickle about fashion, soon tiring of clothes and therefore ending up buying more. 'Ah, but we shop around for bargains whereas boys can't be bothered to,' was one girl's sharp comment.

Far and away the most expensive item that parents mentioned as a regular outgoing were shoes. The boys, however, scored here. Our survey showed that boys tend to wear the same pair of shoes all the year round but girls want a variety — plus boots and sandals. Most parents were paying between £14 and £20 for a pair of shoes for their teenage girls or boys — and for feet that are still growing. Ouch! if you're a parent of daughters!

Finally, on clothes, and just to take the smirk off the boys' faces, one mother said, 'I've just spent £125 on a suit for my son. I'd never have to spend that amount on clothes for my daughter. But he needs a suit for going to job interviews, so what can I do?' She also pointed out that she can swap clothes with her daughter. No father so much as swopped a pair of socks with his son! Agreed?

Pocket money

One issue over which parents would fall over backwards in an attempt to be fair and equal was pocket money. How it was spent or saved was a different matter, but all parents expected their children should at least pay for their own entertainments, records, and 'extras'. Interestingly enough, most were prepared to pay for their children's travelling costs. This proved an interesting point — bus fares for boys but car cost (petrol) for girls. 'My Dad won't let me walk home from the bus stop, so I have to be collected,' said Carla. 'That could be three nights a week — and that works out expensive, I suppose.' But is this typical?

Part-time jobs

While most parents who were questioned wouldn't force their children to take part-time jobs, they did expect them to pay for things like 'luxury' clothes and holidays once they did get one.

It seems, also, that girls can find part-time work more easily than boys (which, of course, means that many girls become less of an expense to their parents sooner than boys). 'And they generally get better paid part-time jobs,' complained Alastair. 'For example, a Saturday shop job!' Also, girls' part-time jobs were thought to be more pleasant than the poorly paid milk and paper rounds which tend to be the staple work diet of boys at school. Do you agree with this?

Food

60 Talking of diets. Get a taste of these quotations:

'My son eats like a horse.'

'Boys always have second helpings while I make do with a sandwich — and it's the same at home.'

'School lunch costs me about 70 pence. I'll have double pie, chips, and beans, three or four pieces of chocolate cake. Oh, and then pie and custard to finish off!'

'I spend 13 pence and have yoghurt and fruit.'

Enough said? Boys lose!

School lunches can be readily costed but meals at home are hidden
70 in the general housekeeping bill. But read the next bit carefully, lads. Time and again parents moaned about their teenage children using the phone 'as if it were their own property', without any thought of the cost. Girls admitted they would ring up a friend 'just for a natter', whereas boys would only ring 'for a purpose'. Boys win!

Conclusion

So, not only is there more expense involved in bringing up children than just buying school uniform, replacing football boots and shelling out pocket money, but age and sex seem to affect costs quite dramatically. Even so, the 'Payday' survey still hasn't sorted out the answer to the question, 'Which cost more — sons or daughters?'

Comprehension and discussion

1 What does 'There is no price tag attached to children' mean?

2 How does the rest of the article go on to say that there is?

3 What is meant by 'the hidden cost of bringing up children'? Give other examples.

4 What was different in the views of teenagers and parents on the bringing up of children?

5 *Clothes*

a What facts are given in this section?
b What opinions are put forward in this section?
c Give your answers to the two questions asked in the section. The first comes at the end of the first paragraph and the second at the end of the section.

6 *Pocket money*

a What is the main statement in this section?
b In what way are boys and girls treated differently?
c There is an example of a 'hidden cost' in this section. What is it?

7 *Part-time jobs*

a What facts are given in the section?
b Does it say that more girls find part-time jobs than boys? Write two or three lines in support of your answer.
c What is your answer to the question at the end of the section?

8 *Food*

a Which topic in this section has nothing to do with the heading?
b What facts are given about the general question of the passage?

9 *Pocket Money*

a How much do you think people of your age should get? Give reasons for your answer.

b What costs should pocket money cover? What things do you think you should not have to pay for out of your pocket money, and who should pay for them?

Activities and research

10 There were two other sections in the article, one on Sport and the other on Hobbies. Collect as much information as you can on the cost of these for boys and girls. Do not forget hidden costs.

11 The article does not answer the question 'Which cost more — boys or girls?' Using the information given here and your own experience, what is your opinion on this?

12 Do you own any items which are insured? Make a list of the types and cost of insurance many families have.

Truants

How often have you stayed away from school when you really could have gone? Most of you probably don't think of yourselves as 'playing truant' but will have stayed away from school without a good reason at least once; maybe because you were ill and had recovered but thought another day at home would be nice; or maybe when you hadn't done some homework and were worried about seeing the teacher concerned. Afterwards, you probably went back to school and carried on as usual. But for some children the 'odd day off' is repeated, and the habit catches on. As you can imagine, as more days
10 are missed, the thought of returning to school gets worse. If this happens, you become part of what many believe is an increasing problem, truancy.

In the last few years, truancy has been given a lot of attention in the press. A recent article in a popular paper talks of 90,000 truants from secondary schools on an average school day (90 or more times the total number of children in your school!). It also suggests that truancy is linked with juvenile crime. The writer's solution to the problem is for more children to be taken to court and for courts to 'impose proper penalties'. Is the number of truants really as many
20 as 90,000 per day? If it is, why are so many young people playing truant? What are the solutions?

How many?

Many people employed in education and social work have tried to find out just how many children actually play truant, but they have no exact answers. Imagine you are trying to work out the number of truants throughout the UK on an average day; you will begin to see the difficulties. To make a start you might arrange for teachers to count the number of absent pupils on all secondary school registers for a particular day in the year. This gives a figure for the number of pupils absent, but you still can't tell how many were genuinely ill
30 and how many were truanting. Nor can you tell the number who

have been in school for registration but mysteriously disappeared later in the day! On the basis of information collected from registers, it is generally thought that about 90% of secondary school pupils are usually in school, or in other words there is a 90% attendance rate. Research workers have tried to estimate the number of truanters among the 10% who are absent. Assessments range from 1% to 5%. In other words if 100 pupils are absent at one secondary school on one day, between 1 and 5 of these could be truants. So it seems as if there would be between 1 and 5 truants per day in a secondary
40   school of 1,000 pupils.

This may add up to the 90,000 mentioned previously but it may not. Hard facts are hard to prove.

Why do people play truant?

Playing truant can have all sorts of consequences for the children concerned, some of which may be harmful. Hanging around the streets and parks can become as boring as school, and boredom can lead to escapades such as glue-sniffing or shoplifting. Truancy can also affect job chances if future employers require a school reference. Once spotted, truancy will lead to an education welfare officer visiting the pupil's home and possibly attendance at a juvenile court.
50   So why do some pupils truant? Are they just 'troublemakers', as many people imagine, or are there some other reasons?

I asked some pupils at one school why they thought people played truant.

'They do it to think they're big. So they can boast to other people.'

'Girls might get a thrill out of sneaking out of the house in jeans and make-up without their parents knowing.'

I then talked to an education welfare officer, whose job is to visit the homes of truants, about her experience of the causes of truancy. She emphasised there was no such thing as an 'average truant' and
60   talked about three different children:

Pamela

Pamela was eleven and had recently started at a school which was well-known for its good examination results and unusual maroon uniform. At the end of the first term after starting the school she had a bad cold and had dreaded going back, but she did. Then, as she was the youngest pupil in the school, she had been asked to present a bouquet on Speech Day. She had worried about this until it became the main topic of conversation at home. Eventually, she refused to do it. Pamela then began to be absent from school. She said school assembly was stuffy and made her feel ill, and the headmistress
70   excused her from attending. She then began to have stomach upsets when she had to go to school. Children such as Pamela who, for complex reasons, get very anxious about going to school are described as having 'school phobia'.

Derek

Derek was just fifteen and one of six children living with his parents in a three-bedroomed house. The family was having a hard struggle to manage financially, and the two children older than Derek had been unable to get jobs and were still at home. The money stresses were causing a lot of family rows. Apparently Derek had two weeks
80 off school after an accident, and then found it difficult to go back. His mother said, 'He just won't get up in the morning.' She didn't know what he did in the day, as she was at work, but thought he sometimes went into town and played on 'Space Invaders'. His father had tried threatening him, but Derek was bigger than his father. Derek himself had said little about why he stayed away from school. He did say he kept trying to go back but felt he couldn't help himself now. He thought the teachers were all right. His form-teacher had pointed out that his school attendance could affect his job prospects, but Derek thought this wasn't true. In any case, one of his older
90 brothers had passed his exams and he still couldn't get a job.

Cathy

Cathy was fourteen and living at home with her mother and sister in a small flat. Her mother stressed that she was 'all right at home'. She explained that she often allowed Cathy to stay off school when she said she felt ill, and that perhaps, as a single parent, she was inclined to be anxious about her daughter. In any case, her mother felt Cathy was not a child, but a grown woman, and she couldn't make her do things any longer. Cathy herself said that she hated school and particularly one teacher who 'picked on her'. The last time she had gone to school the teacher had yelled at her to get out
100 because she looked like a 'wild animal' (Cathy was a 'punk rocker' and had stripes in her hair). Cathy then had to sit in the corridor for half the day, and she thought that was a waste of time. She also thought a lot of lessons were 'silly'. The most important thing in her life was her boyfriend and they wanted to get married as soon as possible.

People who have investigated the causes of truancy have considered not just three cases, but thousands, and they will have been given much more information than I have been able to provide about Pamela, Derek and Cathy. Other reasons for truancy which
110 crop up regularly are: bullying at school, difficulty in making friends at school, changing schools frequently and poverty at home. In many cases, children, particularly girls, turn out to be kept at home by their parents to look after younger children when no-one else can be at home. This is called 'condoned truancy'. Research workers have also found that truancy is much more common among children with fathers in manual jobs. It is also more common (6 or 7 times higher) in families where parents want the children to leave school 'as soon as possible' rather than stay on; this suggests parents' views on school are a very important influence on pupils playing truant.

Comprehension and discussion

1 Are the examples given in the first lines strictly speaking examples of truanting?

2 Say in your own words what you think truanting is. What other terms are used in your area for playing truant?

3 What facts are given about the number of pupils playing truant?

4 What guesses are made about the number?

5 Why do the Attendance Registers of a school not tell us how many pupils are playing truant?

6 *Pamela*

a Was Pamela a truant? Give reasons for your answer.
b Make a list of the ways in which her dislike for school became greater.
c What is your opinion of Pamela's problem?

7 *Derek*

a Do you think that Derek's mother and father are all that bothered about his truanting? Give reasons for your answer.
b What explanation is given for his truanting?
c What do you think about it?

8 *Cathy*

a What is the difference between Cathy's attitude to the teachers and Derek's?
b How did Cathy's mother encourage her to stay off school?
c Which words in the last paragraph of the full extract describe the attitude of Cathy's mother?

Writing

9 What other reasons for truanting are given in the article? List them and after each one write two or three lines showing what you think about it as a reason for truancy.

Further work and discussion

10 Who are the people who worry about pupils playing truant and why do they?

11 Why is it difficult to describe the 'average truant'?

12 The passage leaves out any answer to the question 'What can be done about it?' What suggestions have you to make?

13 Parents may be brought to court and fined if their children do not attend school. Do you think this is fair and should parents be blamed if children play truant?

14 Describe actions from your own life when you tried successfully or unsuccessfully to stay off school.

15 Write a similar article on another problem, for example, smoking. Try to get as many facts as you can; present the actual opinions of people. Take at least three people that you know and give similar profiles, as for Cathy, Derek etc. It will make the article more interesting if one person used to smoke and has given it up, another person would like to give it up, and the third person does not intend to give it up.

Information by Diagrams, Statistics and Sketches

The following are examples which we meet in everyday life of the different ways in which we may receive information. Study the information carefully, then answer the questions on them.

Cricket League tables

The two tables are the League positions of county cricket teams at the end of the same season. They refer to different types of competition. In the County Championship each game lasts for three days and both sides have two innings. Points are awarded not only for winning or drawing but also for good batting and bowling performances. These are shown under the heading 'Bonus pts'. For the John Player League the game lasts one day and each side bowls 40 overs. The side which scores the most runs from the 40 overs wins. The numbers in brackets after the names refer to the position in that League table in the previous year. Other abbreviations used are: P = Games Played; W = Games Won; D = Games Drawn; NR = No Result, mainly because of rain.

JOHN PLAYER LEAGUE

Yorkshire win on the higher number of away wins – five to Somerset's three.

	P	W	L	NR	Tie	Pts
Yorks (16)	16	10	3	3	0	46
Somerset (9)	16	10	3	3	0	46
Kent (4)	16	8	3	5	0	42
Sussex (1)	16	9	5	2	0	40
Hampshire (5)	16	9	6	1	0	38
Derbyshire (12)	16	7	5	4	0	36
Essex (5)	16	7	5	4	0	36
Lancashire (10)	16	5	5	5	1	32
Middlesex (2)	16	7	7	2	0	32
Glamorgan (10)	16	6	8	2	0	28
Leicestershire (3)	16	4	7	5	0	26
Surrey (12)	16	4	7	5	0	26
Worcestershire (15)	16	4	7	2	3	26
Gloucestershire (14)	16	4	8	4	0	24
Northamptonshire (8)	16	5	10	1	0	22
Nottinghamshire (5)	16	4	9	2	1	22
Warwickshire (17)	16	4	9	2	1	22

SCHWEPPES COUNTY CHAMPIONSHIP

	P	W	L	D	Bonus pts Bt	Bl	Pts
Essex (7)	24	11	5	8	69	79	324
Middlesex (1)	24	11	4	9	60	72	308
Hampshire (3)	24	10	2	12	62	71	289
Leicestershire (2)	24	9	3	12	52	81	277
Warwickshire (17)	24	10	3	11	52	64	276
Northamptonshire (9)	24	7	4	13	63	77	252
Kent (13)	24	7	4	13	68	70	250
Surrey (5)	24	7	4	13	65	70	247
Derbyshire (11)	24	7	5	12	46	65	219
Somerset (6)	24	3	7	14	57	75	180
Sussex (8)	24	3	10	11	50	72	170
Gloucestershire (15)	24	3	8	13	56	61	165
Lancashire (12)	24	3	4	17	56	61	165
Nottinghamshire (4)	24	3	10	11	39	62	149
Glamorgan (16)	24	2	10	12	45	64	141
Worcestershire (14)	24	2	11	11	43	54	129
Yorkshire (10)	24	1	5	18	45	64	125

Hampshire & Derbyshire totals include 12pts for wins in 1 innings matches. Gloucestershire and Lancashire finished 12th equal.

County Championship

1 If each team plays home and away against another county, how many counties does any one team not play during the season? Which figures give this information?

2 Which team could best say 'Our bowlers did very well but our batsmen have not done well'?

3 Which team made the most improvement from the previous year and which team did much worse than in the previous year?

4 Lancashire lost only four games, one fewer than Essex. Essex came top. How do you account for the great difference in their positions?

John Player League

5 Yorkshire and Somerset gained the same number of points. How were Yorkshire declared the champions?

6 From the figures given, work out the number of points gained from a Win, a No Result and a Tie.

7 Which team made the greatest improvement over the previous year?

8 If close finishes are exciting, which team had a very exciting season and against which teams did they have these games?

9 Which counties had the fewest games affected by rain?

Both Leagues

10 What is remarkable about Yorshire's position in both tables? Can you account for it in any way?

11 Write a very short paragraph showing how teams can have very different results according to the type of cricket played?

Cost of Christmas

	£	£
Turkey, 14 lb, fresh	7.00	12.88
Mince pies, 6	12p	49p
Christmas pud, 1½ lb	34p	1.08
Christmas cake, 40 oz	90p	5.35
Brussels sprouts, 1½ lb	12p	51p
Potatoes, 3 lb	7½p	48p
½ lb of choclts	40p	1.29
Assrtd nuts, ½ lb cookd	17p	1.75
Christmas tree, 5 ft	60p	7.50
Tree lights	99p	7.99
Tinsel	60p	1.98
Christmas crackers	49p	2.19
Bottle of gin	2.45	6.39
Bottle of whisky	2.39	6.79
Bottle of brandy	4.44	9.49
Pint of beer	19p	62p
24 Christmas cards	60p	4.00
5 shts wrapping papr	15p	60p
Postage, first × 24	84p	3.84
Toys and games	10.95	31.12
Parcel post, 4 × 2 kilos	1.08	8.00
Total	34.89½	114.34

The list above shows how the prices of typical Christmas items have increased over ten years. The later total (£114.34) was about $3\frac{1}{3}$ times the earlier cost.

1 Which two items showed the biggest average increase and which two the lowest?

2 The list is meant to show what an average family with two children might spend at Christmas.
a Is there anything in it which you think could easily have been left out?
b Is there anything missing which you think should have been included?

3 Take a selection of the items and show how much they cost today. Write a short paragraph showing how the prices have changed.

4 Make a list of the items your family bought specially for Christmas or another religious festival.
a How does it differ from the list here?
b Find out how much items cost and write an article with the title 'The Cost of . . . .'

5 Look at the diagram below which gives the list of items on which a family spends money.

a Copy out the diagram and insert as many of the costs as you can.

b Make a similar diagram for the items on which you spend money, e.g. sweets, comics etc.

SPENDING	DAILY	WEEKLY	MONTHLY	QUARTERLY	ANNUALLY
Rent					
Rates					
Holiday					
HP payments					
Gas					
Christmas expenses					
Fares to work					
Lunches					
Magazines and newspapers					
Food					
Clothing					
Car insurance					
Road Tax					
TV Licence					
Cigarettes/ alcohol					
Hairdressing					
Dry cleaning					
Household repairs					
Mortgage repayments					
Insurance on house and contents					
Life assurance					
Electricity					

Washing instructions

1 The figures below are often attached to articles of clothing. They summarise the way the article should be washed and possibly ironed. Study them closely and then work out what examples A–D on page 24 mean. Write out the instructions for each example in clear English.

2 Most jeans are made out of cotton. What other information would you need before you could wash them properly?

3 Using the sketches on page 24 which show how to wash woollens, write a short article explaining what you should and should not do. Give examples of what can go wrong.

4 Describe how you would wash and dry a full set of football/hockey kit.

 White cotton and linen articles without special finishes

 Cotton, linen or rayon articles without special finishes where colours are fast at 60°C

 White nylon; white polyester/cotton mixtures

 Coloured nylon; polyester; cotton and rayon articles with special finishes; acrylic/cotton mixtures; coloured polyester/cotton mixtures

 Cotton, linen or rayon articles where colours are fast at 40°C, but not at 60°C

Wash Tub Symbol

 This indicates that the article can be washed safely either by machine or hand. The figure which appears above the waterline in the tub represents the full washing process and the figure below the waterline represents the water temperature. The symbol may be accompanied by a written description of the process.

Dry cleaning

Normal goods dry cleanable in all solvents.

Normal goods dry cleanable in perchloroethylene, white spirit, Solvent 113 and Solvent 11.

Normal goods dry cleanable in white spirit and Solvent 113.

Drying

Articles can be tumble-dried.

Do not tumble dry as for example articles containing rubber-like articles, and most wool knitwear.

 Acrylics; acetate and triacetate, including mixtures with wool; polyester/wool blends

 Wool, including blankets and wool mixtures with cotton or rayon; silk

 Silk and printed acetate fabrics with colours not fast at 40°C

 Cotton articles with special finishes capable of being boiled but requiring drip drying

 Articles which must not be machine washed (see garment label for manufacturer's instructions)

 Do not wash

 A hand in the wash tub indicates that the article must not be washed by machine. The appropriate hand wash instructions, taken from the appropriate process, may be added in a box alongside the symbol.

Chlorine bleaching

A triangle containing the letters 'Cl' indicates that the article may be treated with *chlorine bleach*. The symbol does not apply to other types of bleach.

Ironing

The temperatures shown in brackets are the maximum sole plate temperatures indicated by the dots in the symbol.

HOT (210°C) Cotton, linen, rayon or modified rayon.

WARM (160°C) Polyester mixtures, wool.

COOL (120°C) Acrylic, nylon, acetate, triacetate, polyester.

 Symbols crossed out with the St. Andrew's cross indicate that garments *must not* be subject to that particular treatment as it would be detrimental to fabric.

A

	MACHINE	HAND WASH
4/50	Hand-hot medium wash	Hand-hot
	Cold rinse. Short spin or drip-dry	
	DO NOT USE CHLORINE BLEACH	
	WARM	
	DRY CLEANABLE	

C

	MACHINE	HAND WASH
2/60	Hot maximum wash	Hand-hot
	Spin or wring	

DO NOT USE CHLORINE BLEACH   HOT   DRY CLEANABLE

B

7/40   ⬜   ⬜   iron   Ⓟ

D

5/40   ⬜   ⬜   iron   Ⓟ

How to wash woollens

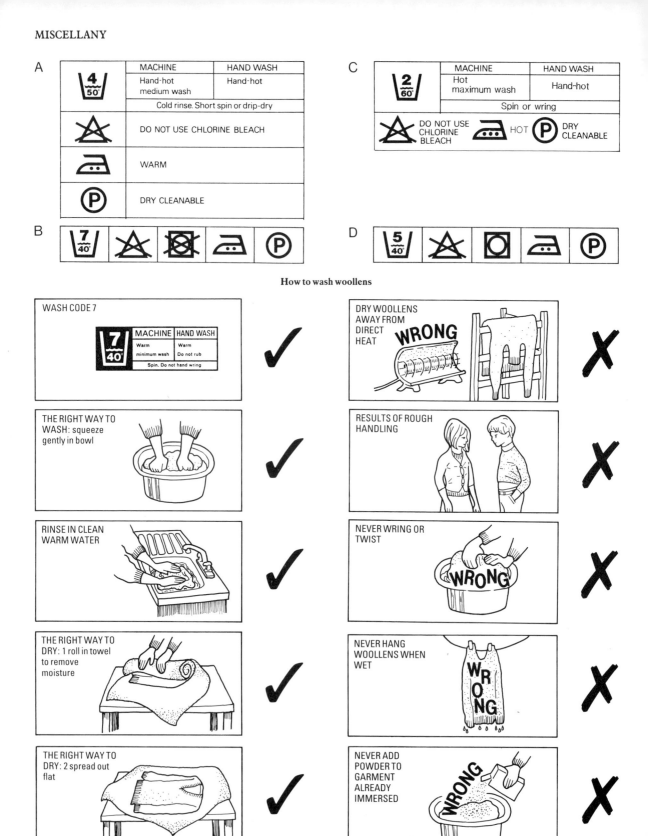

WASH CODE 7

	MACHINE	HAND WASH
7/40	Warm minimum wash	Warm Do not rub
	Spin. Do not hand wring	

✓

THE RIGHT WAY TO WASH: squeeze gently in bowl ✓

RINSE IN CLEAN WARM WATER ✓

THE RIGHT WAY TO DRY: 1 roll in towel to remove moisture ✓

THE RIGHT WAY TO DRY: 2 spread out flat ✓

DRY WOOLLENS AWAY FROM DIRECT HEAT — WRONG ✗

RESULTS OF ROUGH HANDLING ✗

NEVER WRING OR TWIST — WRONG ✗

NEVER HANG WOOLLENS WHEN WET — WRONG ✗

NEVER ADD POWDER TO GARMENT ALREADY IMMERSED — WRONG ✗

2 Description

Contents

First Oysters

We had a very nice time at the oyster beds, and were allowed to go with an old man who only spoke French to catch our own in a thing like a big wire shrimping net. The water in the beds was so clear, and so shallow, that you could see the oysters quite plainly, lying all over the sandy bottom, like fat buns. Some had green seaweed growing on them, some were very small indeed, and some were really very big. We carried them back to the table in a wooden bucket and the parents cheered and seemed delighted and made us sit down together as if it were a sort of party. Which in a way it was, all of
10 us together and in the sunshine and so happy. Our father said that as it would be our first oysters we should be allowed a little glass of wine to have with them, and when Lally looked a bit put out he said that it was a celebration to have your first oyster and it was like launching a ship: you couldn't do it without a little wine.

So the glass jugs of wine arrived at the table, and lemonade for Paul, who was the youngest and didn't have wine or oysters yet, and then the big plates arrived surrounded with seaweed and piled high with oysters all opened and sparkling in the sun. My sister went white when she saw them.
20 'They're raw,' she hissed.

'I know. That's how you eat them.'

'Raw?'

'Yes. Sometimes they get cooked.'

'Alive? Her voice was almost a wail and Angelica and Beth looked at her with a start and then at the great plates of oysters before them.

'They can't be alive!' said Angelica. 'It's like being a cannibal!' Then big bowls of cut lemons and bottles of vinegar were plonked on the wooden table and all the parents started to stretch out for the food. My sister sat shocked into silence while everyone except Lally
30 and Amy raised their glasses in a toast and cried 'Bon appetit!' No one took any notice after that, on purpose, and just got on with the eating part. Our father said to me to watch how he did it with a fork, while Uncle John just took up the whole shell and emptied everything into his mouth.

Dirk Bogarde
A Postillion Struck by Lightning

The most noted Restaurant in the World for Oyster and Lobster

20 Mount Street
Mayfair·
London·W.1.

Scott's

Devised by
PHILIP LAWLESS
Drawings by
DONALD E. GREEN

SAM SCOTT - WORLD CHAMPION OYSTER OPENER
Sam, who began opening oysters in SCOTTS OYSTER BAR in 1938, and is now recognised as the world's most experienced Oyster opener, demonstrates his method here for you.

MUSCLE
BEARD
FLAT (TOP)
FRINGE
DEEP SIDE
HINGE

Approach with Extreme Caution. To begin, you should protect the hand with a cloth or glove.

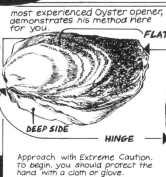

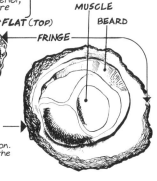

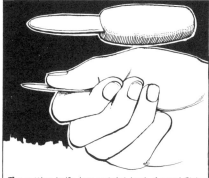

The oyster knife is a special tool. A good Fishmonger or Hardware store should be able to supply one. **Grip** the knife **firmly** in the hand keeping your thumb well down on the blade.

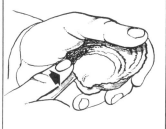

Grip the oyster, deep side in the palm of your hand, insert the knife at the hinge end.

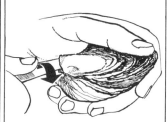

With pressure from both hands lever and twist the knife between the hinge until it separates.

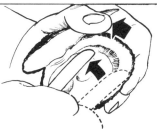

Having broken the hinge, slide the knife from right to left in circular fashion to the far side of the oyster keeping the blade close to the top shell to sever the muscle.
The flat shell is then lifted off and discarded revealing a juicy defenceless oyster.

Reverse the position of the oyster in your hand so from the fringe you insert the knife to cut the meat from shell. Turn the meat over to display the oyster at its best.

ALWAYS serve on the deep side to retain the natural juices.
IF the meat is **dried up** and **curled or** if there is a **bubble** on the deep side **DO NOT SERVE.**

WHAT TO SERVE
A little brown bread and butter Lemon juice, Tabasco Sauce, Chilli Vinegar or plain vinegar to choice.

WHAT TO DRINK
Chablis, Macon or Muscadet.
Guinness or Champagne as individual drinks or mixed to make Black Velvet.

Scott's Telephone: 01- 629 5248

Comprehension and discussion

1 Explain how the oysters were caught.
2 Why was it possible to see the oysters quite plainly?
3 In one sentence, explain how the oysters were carried back to the table.
4 Why did the father think the children should have a glass of wine with their first oysters?
5 Paul could not have wine and oysters. Why was this?
6 List the names of the girls at the oyster party. Which one do you think was the sister?
7 Give two reasons why the sister was upset when she saw the oysters.
8 In one sentence, say which two members of the party did not raise their glasses in the toast.
9 Explain the two different ways of eating oysters.

Summing up

10 Tell the story of this party in not more than 100 of your own words.

Writing

11 Write a description of a school or family lunch. Start by making a list of the sights, sounds and smells of the lunchtime and then organise the list into a definite shape. A good way would be to write a paragraph on each of the senses in turn.
12 Write about a time when you were given food that you could not bring yourself to eat. Tell where it happened, describe the food, and say exactly how you felt.

Oral ideas

13 *Individual talk* Describe any seafood meal you have enjoyed.

Language in use

14 Explain what the following mean in the passage:

   oyster beds (line 1)   celebration (line 13)   launching a ship (line 14) cannibal (line 26)   plonked (line 27) bon appetit (line 30)

15 Read this short description from *A Kid for Two Farthings*:

   Near Alf's stall there was a jellied eel stand with a big enamel bowl of grey jellied eels, small bowls for portions, a large pile of lumps of bread, and three bottles of vinegar. There were also orange and black winkles in little tubs, and large pink whelks. People stood around shaking vinegar on to their eels and scooping them up with bread.

   The writer, Wolf Mankowitz, has picked out in simple language what he could see at the jellied eel stand: a big enamel bowl of eels, small bowls for portions, a large pile of bread and three bottles of vinegar. He has also made the description more attractive by using colours: grey, orange, black and pink.

   Use the same method to write a short description of your local fish and chip or take away shop.

Summarisation

16 Study page 27 with care and then in not more than 80 words explain how to open an oyster.

A Bride Comes Home

Meanwhile the horses jogged along a very bad road. It was getting cooler. A bird whistled, a long sad note. 'What bird is that?' She was too far ahead and did not hear me. The bird whistled again. A mountain bird. Shrill and sweet. A very lonely sound.

She stopped and called, 'Put your coat on now.' I did so and realised that I was no longer pleasantly cool but cold in my sweat-soaked shirt.

We rode on again, silent in the slanting afternoon sun, the wall of trees on one side, a drop on the other. Now the sea was a serene blue, deep and dark.

We came to a little river. 'This is the boundary of Granbois.' She smiled at me. It was the first time I had seen her smile simply and naturally. Or perhaps it was the first time I had felt simple and natural with her. A bamboo spout jutted from the cliff; the water coming from it was silver blue. She dismounted quickly, picked a large shamrock-shaped leaf to make a cup, and drank. Then she picked another leaf, folded it, and brought it to me. 'Taste. This is mountain water.' Looking up smiling, she might have been any pretty English girl and to please her I drank. It was cold, pure and sweet, a beautiful colour against the thick green leaf.

She said, 'After this we go down then up again. Then we are there.' . . .

Soon the road was cobblestoned and we stopped at a flight of stone steps. There was a large screw pine to the left and to the right what looked like an imitation of an English summer house — four wooden posts and a thatched roof. She dismounted and ran up the steps. At the top a badly cut, coarse-grained lawn and at the end of the lawn a shabby white house. 'Now you are at Granbois.' I looked at the mountains purple against a very blue sky.

Perched up on wooden stilts the house seemed to shrink from the forest behind it and crane eagerly out to the distant sea. It was more awkward than ugly, a little sad as if it knew it could not last. A group of negroes were standing at the foot of the veranda steps. Antoinette ran across the lawn and as I followed her I collided with a boy coming in the opposite direction. He rolled his eyes, looking alarmed and went on towards the horses without a word of apology. A man's voice said, 'Double up now, double up. Look sharp.' There were four of them. A woman, a girl and a tall, dignified man were together. Antoinette was standing with her arms round another woman. 'That was Bertrand who nearly knocked you down. That is Rose and Hilda. This is Baptiste.'

The servants grinned shyly as she named them.

'And here is Christophine who was my da, my nurse long ago.'

Jean Rhys
The Wide Sargasso Sea

Comprehension and discussion

1 Why did the writer suddenly become cold in his sweat-soaked shirt?
2 What could be seen on either side as the horses jogged along the very bad road?
3 In one sentence, say what acted as the boundary of Granbois.
4 How was the mountain water tapped?
5 Tell how we know there was an echo in the mountains.
6 Why did the road become cobblestoned?
7 What made the house look sad and ugly?
8 In one sentence, explain why steps were needed to get to the veranda of the house.
9 What was the name of the writer's bride?
10 Name the five servants.
11 Write *two* sentences about either the appearance or the character of (a) the bride, and (b) her husband.

Oral ideas

12 *Individual talks* Tell about any journey you have made to a place that was strange to you.

Language in use

13 This passage comes from R M Ballantyne's book, *Martin Rattler* and is divided into six paragraphs. Add capital letters where necessary and punctuate each paragraph.
a presently a band of young girls came laughing and singing along the road they were dressed in pure-white their rich black tresses being uncovered and ornamented with flowers and what appeared to be bright jewels
b hallo exclaimed martin gazing after them what splendid jewels surely these must be the daughters of very rich people
c the girls seemed to blaze with jewels which not only sparkled in their hair but fringed their white robes and were worked round the edges of their slippers so that a positive light shone around their persons and fell upon the path like a halo
d these jewels said the hermit were never polished by the hands of men they are fire flies
e fire flies exclaimed martin and burney together
f yes they are living fire flies the girls often catch them and tie them up in little bits of gauze and put them as you see on their dresses and in their hair to my mind they seem more beautiful than diamonds sometimes the indians when they travel at night fix fire flies to their feet and so have good lamps to light their path
14 What am I being compared to in each of the following?

e.g. *comparison* I bounced into the classroom.
answer the writer is being compared to a ball.

a I sailed through the examination.
b I bridged the gap between breakfast and lunch with biscuits.
c I skipped English yesterday afternoon.
d I exploded when I was given additional homework.
15 Adjectives are probably the most important word in any passage of description. Pick out six adjectives in *A Bride Comes Home* and say how well they are used.
16 Make out a list of adjectives to use in the description of each of the following:

a Sunday at home   the journey to school
your best friend   getting up in the morning

Activities and research

17 *A Bride Comes Home* tells how it feels as a person nears a place he has never seen before. Most of us have had the same kind of feeling when we go to a new school or move to a new area or go on holiday. Write about a time when this happened to you. Describe your feelings as well as the scene.
18 Look at the picture opposite. Write a careful description of the scene after you have made notes about all the details you see.

The Gun

There it was, the most beautiful-looking weapon I ever saw. Beautiful and deadly-looking.

The holster and filled cartridge belt were of the same soft black leather as the boots tucked under the bunk, tooled in the same intricate design. I knew enough to know that the gun was a single-action Colt, the same model as the Regular Army issue that was the favourite of all men in those days, and that oldtimers used to say was the finest pistol ever made.

This was the same model. But this was no Army gun. It was black, almost blue black, with the darkness not in any enamel but in the metal itself. The grip was clear on the outer curve, shaped to the fingers on the inner curve, and two ivory plates were set into it with exquisite skill one on each side.

The smooth invitation of it tempted your grasp. I took hold and pulled the gun out of the holster. It came so easily that I could hardly believe it was there in my hand. Heavy like father's, it was somehow much easier to handle. You held it up to aiming level and it seemed to balance itself into your hand.

It was clean and polished and oiled. The empty cylinder, when I released the catch and flicked it, spun swiftly and noiselessly. I was surprised to see that the front sight was gone, the barrel smooth right down to the end, and that the hammer had been filed to a sharp point.

Why should a man do that to a gun? Why should a man with a gun like that refuse to wear it and show it off? And then, staring at that dark and deadly efficiency, I was again suddenly chilled, and I quickly put everything back exactly as before and hurried out into the sun.

Jack Schaefer
Shane

Comprehension and discussion

1 In one sentence, explain the boy's feelings towards the gun.
2 What makes us think that the holster, the belt and the boots were a matching set?
3 How do we know the gun was popular and widely used?
4 Tell in your own words why the boy thought, although the gun was the same model, it was not an Army gun.

5 Why was the gun easier to handle than the one belonging to the boy's father?
6 Explain how we know that the owner of the gun was an expert gunman.
7 Write out the following in your own words:
   a 'tooled in the same intricate design'
   b 'exquisite skill'
   c 'smooth invitation of it tempted your grasp'
8 Tell in your own words what impression the writer has tried to give of this gun.

Summing up

9 Say in one paragraph what this passage is about.

Writing

10 Write a description of one of the following in the same way as the passage:
   a a wedding dress
   b any car, train, ship or aircraft
   c a favourite personal possession
   d a famous animal or a pet
11 Describe a typical Western hero or heroine.
12 The action of a story is carried on in a particular place or setting. Describe the kind of setting that one sees over and over again in Western films or reads in Western stories.

Oral ideas

13 *Individual talks* Bring into the classroom any small machine from either home or another part of the school. Describe the machine to the class and then explain how it works.
14 *Group discussion* There is no better film on television than a Western.

Activities and research

15 Read two or three cowboy novels or stories and say which of them you like best. Write a paragraph explaining why you liked it.
16 Make a collection of pictures from magazines and newspapers, and, choosing extracts from poetry, prose and song, make either a folder of work, a booklet or a classroom exhibition about the Wild West.
17 Make a short dictionary of cowboy words.
18 Write a careful description of the cowboy in the picture opposite.

Lok

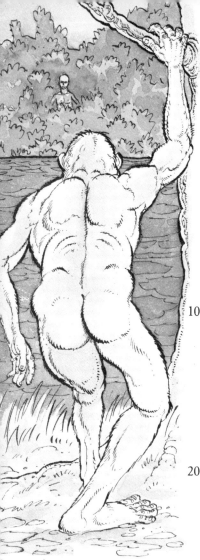

In this passage, a caveman called Lok is attacked by a man from another tribe. He has never seen the weapon before so he cannot call it by its real name. Instead, he describes it in terms of things he knows.

The bushes twitched again. Lok steadied by the tree and gazed. A head and a chest faced him, half-hidden. There were white bone things behind the leaves and hair. The man had white bone things above his eyes and under the mouth so that his face was longer than a face should be. The man turned sideways in the bushes and looked at Lok along his shoulder. A stick rose upright and there was a lump of bone in the middle. Lok peered at the stick and the lump of bone and the small eyes in the bone things over the face. Suddenly Lok understood that the man was holding the stick out to him but neither
10 he nor Lok could reach across the river. . . . The stick began to grow shorter at both ends. Then it shot out to full length again.
    The dead tree by Lok's ear acquired a voice.
    'Clop!'
    His ears twitched and he turned to the tree. By his face there had grown a twig: a twig that smelt of other, and of goose, and of the bitter berries that Lok's stomach told him he must not eat. This twig had a white bone at the end. There were hooks in the bone and sticky brown stuff hung in the crooks. His nose examined this stuff and did not like it. He smelled along the shaft of the twig. The leaves on the
20 twig were red feathers and reminded him of goose. He was lost in a generalised astonishment and excitement.

William Golding
The Inheritors

Comprehension and discussion

1 Name the 'upright stick' that the man held out to Lok.
2 Explain what was happening when the stick grew shorter at both ends and then shot out to full length again.
3 What was the 'twig' that suddenly 'grew' out of the tree by Lok's face?
4 To Lok, the twig smelt of 'the other'. What do you think this was?
5 Give the proper name for the bone at the end of the twig.
6 On that bone there were hooks. What were these for?
7 Sticky brown stuff hung in the crooks. What was it and from what was it made?
8 What made the ears of Lok twitch?

9 Why did the man turn sideways in the bushes and look at Lok along his shoulder?
10 Explain what you think were the 'white bone things' above the man's eyes and under his mouth.

Language in use

11 Write out the passage putting in *all* the correct names that Lok did not know.
12 Compare your version in plain English with that of the writer. Explain why one version is better than the other.
13 In his novel, *A Clockwork Orange*, Anthony Burgess invented an underworld language for a criminal teenage boy. The language used slang from America,

Europe and Russia. Turn this passage from the novel into ordinary spoken English.

the next morning I woke up at oh eight oh oh hours, my brothers, and as I felt shagged and fagged and fashed and bashed and my glazzies were stuck together real horrorshow with sleepglue, I thought I would not go to school. I thought how I would have a malenky bit longer in the bed, an hour or two say, and then get dressed nice and easy, perhaps even have a splosh about in the bath, and then brew a pot of real strong horrorshow chai and make toast for myself and slooshy the radio, or read the gazetta, all on my oddy knocky. And then in the afterlunch I might perhaps, if I still felt like it, itty off to the old skolliwoll and see what was vareeting in that great seat of gloopy useless learning. O my brothers, I heard my papapa grumbling and trampling and then ittying off to the dyeworks where he rabbited, and then my mum called in a very respectful goloss as she did now I was growing up big and strong.

'It's gone eight, son. You don't want to be late again.' So I called back: 'A bit of a pain in my gulliver. Leave us be and I'll try to sleep it off and then I'll be right as dodgers for this after.' I slooshied her give a sort of sigh and she said, 'I'll put your breakfast in the oven then, son. I've got to be off myself now.' Which was true, there being this law for everybody not a child nor with child nor ill to go out rabbiting.

Summing up

14 Take your ordinary spoken English version of the Burgess passage and say what it is about in not more than 50 of your own words.

Writing

15 Write a description of Lok watching a tribesman making fire by turning a stick quickly in a hole in a piece of wood. Lok has never seen fire made before and does not know what is happening.
16 Write a story called 'Lok and the Ice Age'. (Cave Man appeared in the early parts of the Ice Age — about 250,000 BC — and used flakes of stone for tools and axes made from flint.)
17 Here is a passage from *Riddley Martin* by Russell Hoban. The book tells of life after a nuclear war and uses a form of English that nobody ever spoke or wrote before. Take the passage and write it out in today's English.

Raining agen it wer nex morning. Theres rains and rains. This 1 wer coming down in a way as took the hart and hoap out of you there wer a kynd of brilyants in the grey it wer too hard it wer too else it made you feal like all the tracks in the worl wer out paths nor not a 1 to bring you back. Wel of coarse they are but it dont all ways feal that way. It wer that kynd of morning when peopl wernt jus falling in to what they done naturel they had to work ther selfs in to it. Seamt like a lot of tea got spilt at breakfas nor the talk wernt the userel hummeling and mummeling there wer some thing else in it. Like when you see litening behynt the clouds.

Activities and research

18 Ask half a dozen adults of *different* ages what they think of the use of slang. Ask also for examples of slang used by them when younger. The results of your study should be given at your lesson.

The Lane

How beautiful the lane is today, decorated with a thousand colours! The brown road, and the rich verdure that borders it, strewed with the pale yellow leaves of the elm, just beginning to fall; hedgerows glowing with long wreaths of the bramble in every variety of purplish red; and overhead the unchanged green of the fir, contrasting with the spotted sycamore, the tawny beech, and the dry sear leaves of the oak, which rustle as the light wind passes through them; a few common hardy yellow flowers (for yellow is the common colour of flowers, whether wild or cultivated, as blue is the rare one), flowers
10 of many sorts, but almost of one tint, still blooming in spite of the season, and ruddy berries glowing through all. How very beautiful is the lane!

Mary Russell Mitford
Our Village

Comprehension and discussion

1 Mary Russell Mitford describes the lane on a particular day. In which of the four seasons was that day?
2 Name the tree which had not changed, in spite of the season.
3 Most of the flowers in the lane were yellow in colour. Which tree had leaves of the same colour?
4 There was a grass verge to the brown road of the lane. From which tree did leaves fall on that verge?
5 Which trees had (a) light brown leaves, and (b) dried up, withered leaves.
6 What could be seen growing in the hedges of the lane?
7 What was it about the berries that made them stand out in the hedgerows?

Language in use

8 These words are taken from the above paragraph. Use a dictionary to find the meaning of each word and then write it down.

verdure   wreaths   bramble   tawny
sear   hardy   cultivated   ruddy

9 *The Lane* is a paragraph. Like all paragraphs it has a beginning, a middle and an end.
The beginning is the topic or key sentence which says what the paragraph is about, i.e.

How beautiful the lane is today, decorated with a thousand colours!

The middle is made up of several groups of words that tell us how and why the lane is beautiful, i.e.

the yellow leaves of the elm, the purplish red bramble, the tawny beech, the yellow flowers etc.

The end is a sentence that sums up the paragraph and is an echo of the key sentence:

How very beautiful is the lane!

Use this method to write a paragraph about a path, a lane or a road you know in either spring or summer.
10 The use of similes will help improve your writing. A simile makes a comparison in the imagination between two things, using the words 'like' or 'as'. However, make

sure you create new ones, so that you do not use those that have been spoken and written over and over again.

Here are ten such tired similes. Write out each one, but replace the words in brackets with something fresher and more interesting.

as brown as (a berry)
as warm as (toast)
as cunning as (a fox)
as white as (snow)
as wise as (an owl)
as like as (two peas)
as green as (grass)
as good as (gold)
as bold as (brass)
as slippery as (an eel)

11 The similes below have been taken from novels, plays and poems. Tell in your own words what each writer was trying to say to the reader.

a He looked thin but strong, like a straight old pine tree in the twilight.

b Her probing look was like a surgeon's knife that tried to cut through my skull to get at the images there.

c But pleasures are like poppies spread —
You seize the flower, its bloom is shed:
Or like the snow falls in the river —
A moment white, then melts for ever.

d The crowds swarmed over the bargain tables like ants at a picnic.

e . . . Then the law to him
Is like a foul black cobweb to a spider.

Writing

12 Write paragraphs of five or six sentences of which these are the topic or key sentences.

a The view from the top of the hill was enchanting.

b It was evening and the last of the sun drenched everything in golden light.

c The air was full of cries, outlandish smells of smoke and animals, dust and excitement.

d It was morning and had been morning for some time when he heard the plane.

e Life in a city has many advantages.

13 Write paragraphs of five or six sentences of which these are the final sentences.

a It is little wonder, therefore, that people are leaving the district.

b These are the qualities I look for in a good book.

c So ended a day of misfortune.

d After this frightening experience, we vowed never to climb a mountain on our own again.

Oral ideas

14 *Individual talk* Imagine you are blind. Tell of what you hear as you make your way down a busy street with your guide-dog.

15 *Group discussion* I could never live in the country. Town life is the only life for me.

Activities and research

16 Give a picture in words of a great storm sweeping over the area in which you live.

17 Describe the growth of any plant you have been able to watch.

18 Choose a scene you know well. It might be near your home or your school, or part of a favourite walk. Write descriptions of the scene in (a) summer, and (b) winter. Try to get into your writing not only the sights, but also the sounds, smells and feelings that the scene suggests.

19 Mary Russell Mitford says that 'yellow is the common colour of flowers, whether wild or cultivated'. Is this true? Are there more yellow flowers than of any other colour? Use your school and public libraries to check her statement. Write a paragraph saying whether or not you think 'yellow is the common colour of flowers' and give your reasons why.

3 Narrative

Contents

The Tiger in the Tunnel

The cutting curved sharply, and in the darkness the black entrance to the tunnel loomed up menacingly. The signal-light was out. Baldeo set to work to haul the lamp down by its chain. The mail train was due in five minutes.

Then suddenly he stood still and listened. The frightened cry of a barking deer, followed by a crashing sound in the undergrowth, made Baldeo hurry. There was still a little oil in the lamp, and after an instant's hesitation he lit the lamp again and hoisted it back into position. Having done this, he walked quickly down the tunnel,
10 swinging his own lamp, so that the shadows leapt up and down the soot-stained walls, and having made sure that the line was clear, he returned to the entrance and sat down to wait for the mail train.

The train was late. Sitting huddled up, almost dozing, he soon forgot his surroundings and began to nod.

A low grunt resounded from the top of the cutting. In a second Baldeo was awake, all his senses alert. Only a tiger could emit such a sound. . . .

For some time there was only silence, even the usual jungle noises seemed to have ceased altogether. Then a thump and the rattle of
20 small stones announced that the tiger had sprung into the cutting.

Baldeo, listening as he had never listened before, wondered if it was making for the tunnel. He did not have to wonder for long. Before a minute had passed he made out the huge body of the tiger trotting steadily towards him. Its eyes shone a brilliant green in the light from the signal-lamp. Flight was useless.

Ruskin Bond

Comprehension and discussion

1 What were the noises Baldeo heard?
2 What notice did he take of them?
3 Why did he walk through the tunnel?
4 What caused the shadows to leap about?
5 How do we know that he soon forgot the earlier noises?
6 At what point did he realise it was a tiger?
7 How did he know that the tiger had jumped on to the railway track?
8 What does 'flight' in the last line mean and why was it useless?
9 *The Situation* is important in most stories. What details make this situation exciting?
10 *Conflict* is also important in action stories. What is the conflict between here and is it evenly matched?

11 *Vocabulary* Verbs and adverbs are important in any action narrative, e.g. curved sharply, moved up menacingly. List verbs and adverbs which you think describe the action well and show what they do to the story.

Writing

12 Write two to three pages which carry on the story. Remember the details of the situation and the time involved. Also note how the short sentences help to make the story move fast and build up excitement.
13 Write a story of your own but different from this one, starting with the words 'Flight was useless; there was no way I could escape.'

Super Cartoons

'Alfie?'

'What?'

'You studying?'

'Yes,' he lied.

'Well, why don't you come down and study in front of the television? It'll take your mind off what you're doing,' his mother called.

He didn't answer. He bent over the sheet of paper on his table. He was intent.

'Did you hear me, Alfie?'

10 'I heard,' he called without glancing up.

'Well, come on down.' She turned and spoke to Alma. 'Who's the announcer that says that on TV? It's some game show. He says, "Come on downnnn," and people come running down the aisle to guess the prices.'

'I don't know, Mom. I don't watch that junk,' Alma said.

'But you know who I'm talking about. Alfie Mason, come on downnnnn!'

Alfie didn't answer. He was drawing a comic strip called 'Super Bird'.

20 In the first square a man was scattering birdseed from a bag labelled 'Little Bird Seed'. In the next square little birds were gobbling up the seeds.

In the third square the man was scattering birdseed from a bag labelled 'Big Bird Seed'. In the next square big birds were gobbling up the seeds.

In the fifth square the man was scattering huge lumps from a bag labelled 'Giant Bird Seed'. In the last square a giant bird was gobbling up the little man.

There was a smile on Alfie's face as he looked at what he had done.

30 At the top of the drawing he lettered in the words *Super Bird*. He was going to do twelve of these super comic strips, he had decided, one for each month. When he got through, he would call it 'Super Calendar'. Maybe he would get it published, and later, when he learned how, he would animate 'Super Bird', make it into a film. Whenever he drew something, he always saw it in motion.

'Alfie?' his mom called again.

'I'm busy, Mom. I'm studying.'

'Well, supper's ready.'

'Oh.'

40 'Come down right now.'

'I am. I just want to get my papers in order. If I leave them in a mess, sometimes I can't. . .' He trailed off.

He now had two strips for his calendar. 'Super Bird' and 'Super Caterpillar'. He didn't know which he liked best. He looked from one to the other, comparing them.

In the first square of 'Super Caterpillar', a giant caterpillar was happily eating New York City. In the second square he was happily eating New York State. In the third he was happily eating the world. In the last square, he was unhappily falling through space, his stomach a big round ball. Alfie was especially pleased with the expression in Super Caterpillar's eyes as he tumbled helplessly through space.

Betsy Byars
The Cartoonist

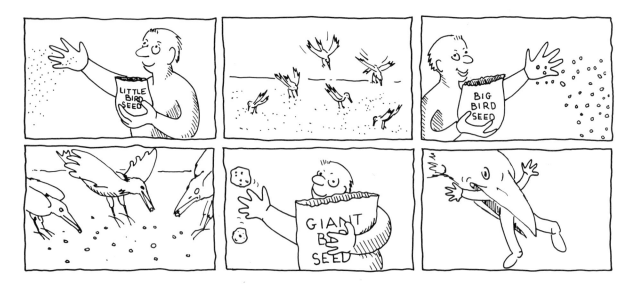

Comprehension and discussion

1 What is unusual about what Alfie's mother tells him to do in lines 5 to 6?
2 In what way is the mother's attitude to TV different from Alfie's and his sister's?
3 What notice does he take of his mother?
4 Why does Alfie smile after he has drawn one of the strips?
5 Describe his attitude towards the cartoons he has drawn.
6 What special skills does he have in drawing cartoons?

Summary

7 What aspects of a story or narrative do his cartoons have?

Language in use

8 Which of the following words describes Alfie? Give your reasons.

cheeky   disobedient   talented   absentminded

9 a Using a dictionary, find out what 'super' means. Select three other words which contain 'super' and use them in sentences.
   b What does 'animated' mean when applied to cartoons? What other meanings does it have? Use it in a sentence with one of the other meanings.
10 Alfie calls his mother 'Mom'. Is this usual in Britain? What does it suggest about his nationality? Try to find out as many other terms for mother and father as you can.

Writing

11 Describe what Alfie's mother is like, particularly her character.
12 Which is Alfie more likely to become, a cartoonist for a paper or for the television?
13 Why do you think cartoons on the television are so popular when they contain so much cruelty? Why do we so easily accept in cartoons that animals can talk?
14 How typical is Alfie's conversation with his mother? Does it happen in your home? Write out a short typical conversation between you and one of your parents on
   a Getting up out of bed
   b Tea's ready!
   c Doing homework
   d Washing up after a meal
15 Try drawing one of Alfie's strip cartoons. Following the examples given, make outlines either in words or sketches of the following:

Super Weed   Super Pupil   Super Fish   Super Custard

The Interview

The person speaking has applied for a job on the railway.

I went straight up to the door and I gave a good firm knock on it.

'Come in,' called a voice.

I turned the door-handle and went in. It was more like a small workshop than an office. There were lots of plans and blueprints around the place, and also some engineer's fine tools hanging from shelves. Mr Bidwell was standing beside his desk. He was a round-faced man and not nearly as frightening as I had imagined. I put on a special big smile for him.

10   'Good morning, sir,' I called out in a loud voice.

'Good morning, laddie,' he said. I could see he was rather pleased at my smiling appearance, as though he wasn't used to people smiling at him.

'I've come for a job, sir,' I said. He was going to say something but I thought it might be better if I said all my piece at once. 'I don't care how low I start, sir. I'll soon work my way up. And what's more, I can start this very minute.'

In that moment I could see that I had won him. He was an elderly man, grown old before his time, I decided, and he wasn't at all the
20 ogre he had been made out to be. He was smiling warmly at me and I realised the job was mine. I pictured myself on the footplate of the Flying Scotsman on my first long trip, with my mum and dad in the first-class compartment behind. . . .

'Now on what job, sir,' I said, 'would you like me to start?'

He hesitated. 'I'm not sure,' he said. 'It's not for me to say, not rightly.'

'Oh, but it is,' I said. 'I'll do anything you tell me.'

He shook his head. 'I think it'd be better,' he said, 'if you were to wait and see Mr Bidwell.'

30   I could hardly believe my ears. 'M-mister who?'

'Mr Bidwell,' he said. 'I'm only the sweeper-up.'

Bill Naughton
A Real Good Smile

Comprehension and discussion

1 What does the opening sentence tell us about the speaker's/narrator's attitude to the interview?

2 What statement encourages the reader to make the same mistake as the narrator?

3 Can you suggest why the narrator made this mistake?

4 How did he try to impress the old man?

5 How did his first mistake make him misinterpret the old man's actions?

Writing

6 Carry on the story after Mr Bidwell comes in. Try to imagine how the speaker felt after he realised the mistake he had made and remember that Mr Bidwell has the reputation of being an ogre.

7 Write a similar account using the following guidelines:

a An angry parent mistaking the school caretaker for a teacher

b A boy/girl meeting a girl/boy whose twin he/she had met at a disco

Appointment in Samarra

There is a well-known legend told in many countries round the
world. Although the details may change the main outline of the story
is always the same. The story is about a wealthy businessman who
was very superstitious and had a great fear of death. He spent much
of his money on expensive medicines and consulted only the best
doctors in the land. He had armed guards with fierce dogs patrolling
the grounds of his large house, and wherever he went he always had
two personal bodyguards.

10   Every day he read his horoscope to make sure that he avoided
danger. However, his love of money was as great as his fear of death.
One day he read in his horoscope that he would have a very
important business meeting which would alter his life and wealth
completely. Thinking that it was another business deal which would
make him a lot of money, he eagerly set out to his office. He parked
his car in the underground car park and as he was leaving it he saw
in the distance a grim-looking figure. The figure came closer and he
recognised that it was Death. He stopped immediately. Death also
stopped and stretched out his arm, pointing his finger at the
businessman. He turned round in terror and ran back to his car. He
20   drove home as fast as he could looking behind him all the time for
fear that Death was following him, but the road was clear. When he
arrived home he told his wife what had happened. She tried to calm
him down but he was gasping and shaking with fear.

    'You are one of the richest men in the country', she said, 'and yet
you behave like a frightened baby. It's all in your imagination. You
have let that horoscope make you imagine things.'

    'That's it,' he cried out. 'That's the meeting it talked about. Well
I've avoided it and I'll make sure I avoid it for the rest of the day.
I'll get as far away from here as I can. I'll go to my brother's house
30   in Samarra and stay there with him until tomorrow, and tomorrow
there'll be a different horoscope for me.'

    In spite of all his wife said he did this and he drove with his two
bodyguards to Samarra which was many miles in the opposite
direction. After he had gone his wife decided to find out for herself
what had happened so she went to the town. There she saw a
road accident in the town centre and standing slightly apart from the
crowd was the figure that she recognised as the one her husband had
seen earlier. She went straight up to him and pointing to the road
accident she said, 'Isn't this the business you have come here for
40   today? Why then did you deliberately frighten my husband this
morning?'

    The figure turned slightly towards her and said, 'I did not mean
to frighten your husband; I was just surprised to see him here. You
see I thought I had an appointment to meet him in Samarra tonight,
so I was amazed to see him here so far away.'

Based on an extract from *Sheppey*,
a play by Somerset Maugham.

Comprehension and discussion

1 What is the main outline of this story?
2 Give examples of the details which could be changed without altering the main outline.
3 Give two reasons why the man read his horoscope every day.
4 How did he misunderstand his horoscope?
5 What did the man think the figure was intending to do when he pointed at him?
6 Show how this mistake was fatal.
7 Why did the businessman try to protect himself? What could he not protect himself against?
8 Why do you think the figure had gone to the town centre?
9 Do you think that the man's horoscope came true or not? Give reasons for your answer.

Writing

10 Do you ever read your own horoscope and do you believe in it?
11 Give examples of your horoscope from different types of papers or magazines and say what you think they mean and whether they give a good guide to the future.
12 What other forms of telling the future are there? Describe each one and say whether you find it reliable or not.
13 What do we mean when we say that a story has a 'twist in the tail'? Write a short story which is about a visit to a fortune teller with a surprise at the end.
14 Write a short article about the superstitions that you and people you know have. Try to explain why people are superstitious.

Language in use

15 Give three adjectives which you think apply to each of the following:
a The businessman
b His wife
c The strange figure
16 Use a dictionary to find out the difference between
a a legend, a myth and a fairy tale;
b astrology and astronomy.

Library work

If you like this sort of story see if your library has books by Roald Dahl or O Henry. Both write short stories with twists in the tail.

"Oh—oh . . . I see the number thirteen. I hope you're not superstitious."

Murder in School

The day began like any other at Bramthorpe College for Girls. . . .

The electric bells sounded throughout the building at a quarter to nine. At that precise moment two doors were opened. Day girls and boarders alike streamed through, directly into the cloakrooms to hang up coats and to change into houseshoes. In seemly fashion — no shouting or running in the corridors was permitted — the young ladies then made their way to their form rooms where monitors collected the exercise books containing the previous evening's written prep.

10   At ten to nine, the second bell sounded. By now the cloakrooms were empty, but just to make sure, the duty mistress of the week visited them, noting carefully any gross untidiness so that the culprits — easily identified by the numbers on the pegs — could be spoken to later. At the same time, the school prefects left their sanctum and went one to each form room. Their job was first, to ensure that the monitors had collected and counted the exercise books and then carried them to the open lockers outside the staff common room, there to be left for the mistresses concerned to collect for marking. Second, to ensure that girls whose first lesson would be elsewhere

20   than in their own form rooms collected from their desks the books that would be needed during the first period. Third, to ensure that every girl took from her desk her Bible and hymn book. Fourth, and finally, to make sure, as soon as the third bell sounded at five to nine, that girls left their form rooms, armed with all the necessary volumes, and made their way to Big Hall for Assembly.

It was all a routine, smooth and practised. Some forms had a long way to go to the hall. The next five minutes, however, allowed plenty of time. In the hall, waiting to receive them, was the duty mistress. Each girl filed to her allotted seat. The prefects sat down the left-

30   hand gangway, each with the form for which she was responsible. While the duty mistress kept order, the prefects counted their charges and noted any empty seats. At two minutes to nine, the other mistresses filed in and up the stairs onto the stage. The one who accompanied the singing removed the all-enveloping dust-cover from the grand piano and took her seat at the instrument. The other mistresses sat down — being careful to remove their hymnals from the seats of their chairs before doing so.

But today there was a difference. The deputy headmistress, Miss Bulmer, did not enter with the rest of her colleagues. Her non-

40   appearance was enough of an incident to cause comment in this well-ordered assembly.

'Where's the Bull?'

'The Bull's got collywobbles — I hope.'

'Quiet. Samantha Ellison . . . and you, Sara Brett . . . you are talking.' The duty mistress was picking out the culprits in her effort to quell the murmur of comment.

Nine o'clock. As the bells sounded, the hall door nearest the stage opened — as it always did — but not, this time, to admit the head-mistress. In her stead came the missing Miss Bulmer.

50   'It's not the Bull who's ill. It's the Old Dutch.'

'The Old Dutch is taking the day off, lucky thing.'

This time the murmurs went unchecked. The duty mistress, her period of policing over, had taken her place among the other mistresses. As everybody rose from their seats at the entry of Miss Bulmer, the excited whispers, by no means lost in the shuffle of feet, continued. Miss Bulmer, grave-faced, walked slowly to the head's rostrum. She spoke no word; made no attempt to quieten the assembly. She stood and faced them, row upon row of youthful faces, and there was something in her attitude which brought them to

60   silence. The whispering died, to be followed by a long moment of completely unbroken quiet. Only then did Miss Bulmer speak.

'Miss Holland,' she said quietly and sadly, 'died during the night.'

Douglas Clark
Golden Rain

Comprehension and discussion

1 What facts show that some of the pupils are boarders?
2 What do the words 'At that precise moment' tell us about the way the school is organised?
3 Make a timetable of events summarising the main action according to the times given.

8.45 –

4 What were the duties of the teachers before Assembly started?
5 What did the prefects (monitors) have to do regarding the homework (i.e. prep)?
6 Write down the sentence in the third paragraph which best describes the way the Assembly was organised.
7 Two nicknames of staff are used. Explain how they got these nicknames.
8 What was the first indication that it was not an ordinary day? How did the girls react to this?

Writing

9 The Headmistress had been found dead, poisoned by something she had eaten the previous evening. The circumstances made it look like murder and not an accident. The murder could have been carried out by one or more of the following:
a pupils
b teaching staff
c non-teaching staff
d an outsider not connected with the school, e.g. a thief
e an outsider connected with somebody in the school
Choose one of these and draw up an outline of the rest of the story.
10 Write out an interview between the police and two or three pupils or two or three staff.
11 Describe the situation at your own school before Assembly starts.
12 Describe the way your own Assembly is conducted and make it lead up to a startling announcement as in this extract.
13 What part does the detailed description of activities and duties play in the lead up to the climax of the announcement?

Keeping Lodgers

The following extract is from a story called The Landlady *concerning Billy who was looking for cheap lodgings in a strange town. He noticed a small guest house with a parrot in the window. The prices advertised were a lot less than he had seen anywhere else. An old lady invited him in and gave him a cup of tea. While she was making it he noticed that there were only two names in the guest book — a Mr Mulholland and a Mr Temple and their names had been entered some years previously.*

Billy started sipping his tea. She did the same. For half a minute or so, neither of them spoke. But Billy knew that she was looking at him. Her body was half-turned towards him and he could feel her eyes resting on his face, watching him over the rim of her teacup. Now and again, he caught a whiff of a peculiar smell that seemed to emanate directly from her person. It was not in the least unpleasant, and it reminded him — well, he wasn't quite sure what it reminded him of. Pickled walnuts? New leather? Or was it the corridors of a hospital?

10   'Mr Mulholland was a great one for his tea,' she said at length. 'Never in my life have I seen anyone drink as much tea as dear, sweet Mr Mulholland.'

    'I suppose he left fairly recently,' Billy said. He was still puzzling his head about the two names. He was positive now that he had seen them in the newspapers — in the headlines.

    'Left?' she said, arching her brows. 'But my dear boy, he never left. He's still here. Mr Temple is also here. They're on the third floor, both of them together.'

    Billy set down his cup slowly on the table, and stared at his
20 landlady. She smiled back at him, and then she put out one of her white hands and patted him comfortingly on the knee.

    'How old are you, my dear?' she asked.

    'Seventeen.'

    'Seventeen!' she cried. 'Oh, it's the perfect age! Mr Mulholland was also seventeen. But I think he was a trifle shorter than you are, in fact I'm sure he was, and his teeth weren't *quite* so white. You have the most beautiful teeth, Mr Weaver, did you know that?'

    'They're not as good as they look,' Billy said. 'They've got simply masses of fillings in them at the back.'

30   'Mr Temple, of course, was a little older,' she said, ignoring his remark. 'He was actually twenty-eight. And yet I never would have guessed it if he hadn't told me, never in my whole life. There wasn't a *blemish* on his body.'

    'A what?' Billy said.

    'His skin was *just* like a baby's.'

    There was a pause. Billy picked up his teacup and took another sip of his tea, then he set it down again gently in its saucer. He waited for her to say something else, but she seemed to have lapsed into another of her silences. He sat there staring ahead of him into the
40 far corner of the room, biting his lower lip.

    'That parrot,' he said at last. 'You know something? It had me completely fooled when I first saw it through the window from the street. I could have sworn it was alive.'

    'Alas, no longer.'

    'It's most terribly clever the way it's been done,' he said. 'It doesn't look in the least bit dead. Who did it?'

    'I did.'

    '*You* did?'

    'Of course,' she said. 'And have you met my little Basil as well?'
50 She nodded towards the dachshund curled up so comfortably in front of the fire. Billy looked at it. And suddenly, he realized that this animal had all the time been just as silent and motionless as the parrot. He put out a hand and touched it gently on the top of its back. The back was hard and cold, and when he pushed the hair to one side with his fingers, he could see the skin underneath, greyish-black and dry and perfectly preserved.

    'Good gracious me,' he said. 'How absolutely fascinating.' He

turned away from the dog and stared with deep admiration at the little woman beside him on the sofa. 'It must be most awfully
60   difficult to do a thing like that.'

'Not in the least,' she said. 'I stuff *all* my little pets myself when they pass away. Will you have another cup of tea?'

'No, thank you,' Billy said. The tea tasted faintly of bitter almonds, and he didn't much care for it.

'You did sign the book, didn't you?'

'Oh, yes.'

'That's good. Because later on, if I happen to forget what you were called, then I can always come down here and look it up. I still do that almost every day with Mr Mulholland and Mr . . . Mr . . .'
70   'Temple,' Billy said. 'Gregory Temple. Excuse my asking, but haven't there been *any* other guests here except them in the last two or three years?'

Holding her teacup high in one hand, inclining her head slightly to the left, she looked up at him out of the corners of her eyes and gave him another gentle little smile.

'No, my dear,' she said. 'Only you.'

Roald Dahl

Comprehension and understanding

1 Describe what Billy's feelings were like as he drank his tea and as he received each piece of information from the lady.
2 What was odd about the smell from the woman?
3 Having read the full extract, what do you think the smell was and why do you think she kept looking at him closely?
4 How do we know that he felt uncomfortable?
5 What does he do to break the feeling of uneasiness?
6 What other information about the house does this then reveal?
7 Billy says 'How absolutely fascinating'. Would you find the information he has just been given fascinating? Give reasons for your answer.

Language in use

8 Look at the tenses of the verbs which refer to Mr Mulholland and Mr Temple in paragraphs 2 and 4. What do they suggest?
9 Look at the meaning of each of the following words and say which of them best describes the smell coming from the woman.

sickly   bitter   pungent   sharp

Can you suggest other words that might be appropriate?

10 In what way is the word 'stared' different from 'looked' and why is it used in line 58?
11 Why did Billy seem to suspect nothing? Pick out the words which describe the old lady and use them in your answer.

Further writing

12 Using the information given, what do you think has happened to the two lodgers?
13 Continue the story in the way it probably turned out. You can use either the 1st person (I) or the 3rd person (he, Billy). Which one gives you the greater freedom of choice for a happy ending?

Library work

Use reference books in the library to find out why the tea tasted of bitter almonds.

Explanation

Contents

The Big Train Ride

*MOSKVA — IRKUTSK — KHABAROVSK —
VLADIVOSTOK*

The Trans-Siberian Railway is the most important railway line in the
Soviet Union because it links the capital Moscow with cities and
towns in Siberia and the Far East. The building of the railway began
in 1891, with work starting from both Moscow and Vladivostok at
the same time. By 1898 the builders had got halfway along the route,
and by 1904 Moscow and Vladivostok had been joined.

At first, the passengers were unable to make the whole journey by
train, but had to travel by boat (or sleigh in winter) across Lake
Baikal. This lake stood in the path of the railway line for a number
of reasons. It is 395 miles long with an average width of 30 miles,
it is the world's deepest lake (max. depth 5,315 feet), and contains
one-fifth of all the fresh water on the earth's surface. The problems
were solved by building a line around the lake, and this was
completed in 1916.

The *Rossiya* (or *Russia*) express of the Trans-Siberian line leaves
daily from Yaroslavl Station in Moscow at 10.10 a.m. This is Train
No. 2 which travels from Moscow to Vladivostok: Train No. 1 is also
called *Rossiya* and comes the other way from Vladivostok to Moscow.

The distance to Vladivostok is 5,810 miles and the journey takes
about 170 hours or seven full days. The same distance can be covered
by air in just over 8 hours. The route covers 7 time-zones, so that
by the time the train reaches the Pacific it is 7 hours ahead of Moscow
time. It has, however, kept to Moscow time throughout, as have the
clocks on all the stations along the route.

The *Rossiya* and its 16 or 17 coaches is hauled by CHS2 and CHS4
electric engines built in Czechoslovakia. Most of the coaches are
sleeper cars designed for long distance travel. The compartments are
roomy, with two berths in first class and four berths in second. There
are washbasins in every first class compartment, whilst second class
coaches have washbasins and toilets at either end. All coaches are
well insulated and in the cold Russian winter a comfortable temperature is maintained inside. Each car has its own conductor who serves
tea, cake and biscuits. There is also a restaurant car where main
meals are served and a radio car to keep the train in touch with the
world outside. The *Rossiya* also carries a library and games such as
chess to help passengers pass the time.

There is no continuous road across Siberia to the Russian Far East,
although work has begun on one. The Trans-Siberian Railway is
therefore the only means of communication that can carry passengers
and heavy freight all the year round from Western Europe to the
Pacific coast of the USSR. There is no railway journey of the same
length anywhere else in the world: it is the big train ride.

Ronald Hawthorne

Comprehension and discussion

1 Why is the Trans-Siberian Railway so important to the Soviet Union?
2 How many years did it take to build a continuous line between Moscow and Vladivostok?
3 Why were the first passengers unable to make the whole journey by rail?
4 Name two cities at which the *Rossiya* stops on its journey from Moscow to Vladivostok.
5 In one sentence, explain the difference between first and second class compartments.
6 What time is it in Vladivostok when the *Rossiya* leaves Moscow?
7 How are the passengers protected from the cold during the winter months?
8 In one sentence, explain the eating arrangements on the train.

Activities and research

9 *The Orient Express* has been made famous by Agatha Christie. Find out what you can about this well-known train and the famous men and women who travelled on her. Write and illustrate a short booklet called *The Orient Express*.
10 The picture on page 53 is of King Edward VII's day saloon, with his smoking room beyond, on the London and North Western Railway's Royal Train of 1903. Describe this superb room on a train as carefully as you can.

Writing

11 Give a vivid description of any trip you have made by train.
12 Look at the picture on the front cover of this book. Write about it in any way you wish.
13 Here is a step-by-step explanation, taken from a rule book issued by the Pullman Car Company of America during its early years, advising train staff on how to take an order for beer and then serve it.

1 Ascertain from passenger what kind of beer is required.
2 Arrange set-up on bar tray in buffet: one cold bottle of beer, which has been wiped, standing upright; glass two-thirds full of finely chopped ice (for chilling purposes — making it a distinctive service); glass; bottle opener; and paper cocktail napkin. Attendant should carry clean glass towel on his arm with fold pointing towards his hand while rendering service.
3 Proceed to passenger with above set-up.
4 Place bar tray with set-up on table (or etc.)
5 Place paper cocktail napkin in front of passenger.
6 Present bottle of beer to passenger displaying label and cap. Return bottle to bar tray.
7 Pour ice from chilled glass into other glass.
8 Open bottle of beer with bottle opener in presence of passenger (holding bottle at an angle), pointing neck of bottle away from passenger; wipe top of bottle with clean glass towel.
9 Pour beer into glass by placing top of bottle into glass, and slide the beer down the side until beer reaches about two inches from the top — then put a collar on the beer by dropping a little in the glass which should now be upright.
10 Place glass containing beer on paper cocktail napkin.
11 Place bottle containing remainder of beer on table before passenger, with label facing him.

Give a similar detailed explanation for a waiter to take an order for your favourite drink and then serve it.

Summing up

14 Tell in 100 of your own words the story of 'the big train ride' for a ten-year-old.

Language in use

15 Arrange the following into four lines of verse and add capital letters and punctuation marks where you feel it necessary.

i know a stingy fellow and his name is farmer grab and he doesn't live so very far away he's more prickly than a thistle and much sourer than a crab and he's duller than a lump of clay

16 Complete these words by adding -*ei* or -*ie*:

bel _ _ ved	defic _ _ nt
th _ _ r	th _ _ ves
perc _ _ ved	fr _ _ ndship
conc _ _ ving	s _ _ zed
n _ _ ghbours	requ _ _ m

17 Complete these words by adding a letter for each dash:

livel _ hood	compar _ tively
acqui _ _ al	persist _ nt
sher _ _	mass _ _ _ ed
picturesq _ _	g _ _ rd
orig _ nal	proc _ _ ded
tr _ _ cherous	r _ ythm
infl _ _ ntial	wakefu _ ness
g _ _ l	

18 Of the following 30 words, half are spelt correctly and the others are misspelt. Separate the right ones from the wrong.

battalion	catarrh	loneliness
persuit	vicious	truely
insistant	anoint	liesure
recommend	superseed	definately
surprise	paralysis	fulfill
wierd	gaiety	inoculate
disappoint	hypocrasy	inimitable
occurred	accomodate	arguement
embarassed	millionaire	procede
heros	desperate	seperate

Oral ideas

19 Make sure you can pronounce these words:

aisle	courteous	diphtheria
amateur	patio	lingerie
laboratory	advertisement	gnawed
blotchy	camellias	nether
evocative	pantomime	suede

Use a dictionary to find the meaning of any word that is not known to you.

A Russian train

Ice Cream

Ice cream is the most popular sweet dish in the world. It first appeared in Europe at a meal for the Roman emperor Nero: not a real ice cream probably, but a dish made from snow and fruit juices.

It was Marco Polo who, in the 13th century, brought to Europe from China a recipe for an ice dessert made with milk. This 'ice cream' became very popular with people of high rank, and the recipe was soon improved by their chefs. An early mention of ice cream in England was at Henry V's Coronation banquet in 1413 when there was 'creme frez' as a third course.

10 Such recipes were kept secret for many years but in time they became available to everyone. In 1846 an easy to carry, hand-operated freezer was invented and people began to make ice cream at home. Ice cream was not made on a large scale, however, until the late 18th century when new methods of refrigeration by machine were invented.

Commercial ice cream is made from cream or butterfat, milk, nonfat milk solids, sugar, stabilisers, flavouring, and sometimes eggs. Butterfat gives the ice cream its creamy flavour and improves the way it feels when tasted. The stabilisers prevent large ice crystals forming 20 during the freezing process, and sugar and the various kinds of flavouring provide sweetness and taste. Natural flavourings such as fruit and nuts give variety.

The world is eating more ice cream today than ever before, and there are well over 200 flavours from which to choose. Some 70 per cent of all ice cream eaten is vanilla flavoured. The second most popular flavour is strawberry, followed by coffee and chocolate. Flavours such as ginger and banana have been tried but have not sold well. Neither have savoury ice creams flavoured with bacon, watercress, potato, cheese or mustard.

30 Products similar to ice cream include sherbert, ice-milk, frozen custard and tortoni. Sherbert is usually made with fruit or fruit juices, sweeteners and small amounts of egg white or milk. Ice-milk contains more nonfat milk solids and less butterfat than ice cream. Frozen custard has all the ingredients of ice cream but with extra amounts of egg or egg yolks. Tortoni is an ice cream made with heavy cream and containing minced almonds, chopped cherries or other fruits.

Three out of every four people in Britain now eat ice cream regularly. On average, each person eats three quarts per year and 40 nearly 3,000 ice cream makers are needed to meet this demand. Blackpool holds the record for the most ice cream eaten each year in any seaside resort, but consumption varies from area to area. Surprisingly, for example, the people in Glasgow eat much more ice cream than those in London. In the long run, however, sales still depend on weather, and a hot summer will make people buy ten times more ice cream than usual.

Rupert Henchard

Comprehension and discussion

1 Explain in one sentence what this passage is about.
2 Why was the recipe for ice dessert brought by Marco Polo from China called 'ice cream'?
3 At which fifteenth-century meal was ice cream served as a third course?
4 In one sentence for each explain what these words mean:
   recipe   dessert   chef   banquet
   commercial   refrigeration
   ingredients   quart   consumption
5 What is meant by the phrase *refrigeration by machine*?
6 How does commercial ice cream get its creamy flavour?
7 Explain in one sentence why stabilisers are used in the making of commercial ice cream.
8 Name any three ice cream flavours that have not become popular.
9 What is added to the ingredients for ice cream in order to make frozen custard?
10 What is the average consumption of ice cream for each of us in one year?

Oral ideas

13 *Individual talks* Explain clearly how to do one of the following:
   a mend a puncture
   b bake a jacket potato
   c use an index
   d play any game
   e operate an electronic machine
   f keep a pet
   g grow a plant
14 *Individual talks* Explain clearly why something is important to you.

Language in use

15 Here are some sentences that can have more than one meaning. Take each sentence and explain the two different meanings it may have.
   a Have you heard how old Mr Chips is?
   b Write your problem on the blackboard and I will go through it with you.
   c If your dog is upset by raw meat then cook it.
   d Caning should be restricted to head-teachers.

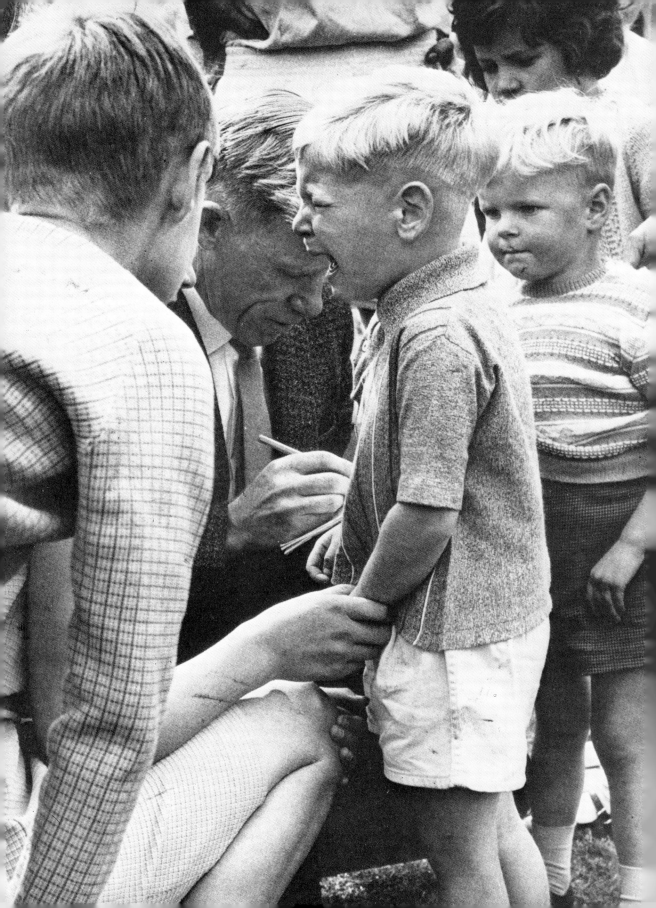

16 Complete the spelling of the following by adding one of these:

ous   eous   ious   uous

riot . . . . . .   tremend . . . . . .
gorg . . . . . .   consc . . . .
obnox . . . . . .   vic . . . .
spontan . . . . . .   superfl . . . . . .
contin . . . . . .   assid . . . . . .
caut . . . . . .   gas . . . .
pernic . . . . . .   ambit . . . . . .

17 There is a silent letter in each of the following words. For each word write down the letter that is not pronounced.

ostler   ghastly   depot
subtle   fastened   wrestler
nestle   aisle   pneumonia
honesty   ballet   apostle
wrinkle   soften   dumbfounded
scissors   psalm   mortgage
resign   rhythm

Coffee granita

Metric	Imperial
4 × 15 ml spoons	*4 tablespoons*
Continental or other	*Continental or other*
strong blend of freshly	*strong blend of*
ground coffee	*freshly ground coffee*
100 g caster sugar	*4 oz caster sugar*
450 ml boiling water	*¾ pint boiling water*

Granita is an Italian water ice which is usually served with whipped cream as a dinner party dessert. It can be made with fruit or coffee and is always served ice cold. Granita is not beaten during freezing and so its texture is coarse and granular — quite different from other water ices and sorbets which have the ice crystals beaten out of them during freezing.

If using the refrigerator, turn it to its coldest setting.

Put the coffee and sugar in a jar and stir in the boiling water. Stir until the coffee and sugar have dissolved, then leave to cool.

Strain the coffee liquid into a freezer container and chill in the refrigerator for at least 30 minutes. Transfer to the freezing compartment of the refrigerator or to the freezer and freeze for at least 2 hours or until completely solid.

Remove the granita from the container, then quickly chop into large chunks with a large strong knife. Return it to the container and freeze again until required. Serve straight from the freezer with whipped cream if liked.

Return the refrigerator to its normal setting.

Keeps for 2 months.

18 Arrange the following into seven lines of verse and add capital letters and punctuation where you feel it necessary.

as i was going to st ives i met a man with seven wives every wife had seven sacks every sack had seven cats every cat had seven kits kits cats sacks and wives how many were going to st ives

Summing up

19 Tell in not more than 100 words what the passage on ice cream is about.

Writing

20 Explain why you like one particular time of the year more than any other.

21 Write an explanation of what is happening in the picture on the opposite page.

22 Write a simple explanation for a young child of why it snows.

23 Tell about an animal that has made your life more enjoyable.

Activities and research

24 Ask five or six adults what they think of the idea of savoury ice cream. If need be invent some flavours. Write down their answers and finish by adding comments of your own.

25 Read the recipe opposite and then answer these questions.

a For what do the metric abbreviations *ml* and *g* stand?

b In one sentence for each, explain the meaning of:

texture   coarse   granular

c Why is the texture of granita coarse and granular?

d What is the Imperial measure equivalent of 450 ml of water?

e Tell in your own words what happens to the *completely solid* granita.

f Write a similar recipe of your own for a tea or chocolate granita.

Timur the Great Lame Man

'Everything I have heard about the beauty of Samarkand is correct, but actually it is more beautiful than I had imagined.'

These are the words of Alexander the Great when first he saw this ancient capital of Asia on his march to India in the fourth century before Christ.

Samarkand is in central Asia, is over 2,500 years old, and has been called *'the gem of the world'*, *'the shining point of the globe'*, and *'the city of famous shadows'*.

It has seen many conquerors like Alexander because of its beauty and its position on the Silk Road. This road was 8,000 miles long and ran from Spain to China. It was used by vast caravans to bring back silk and spices from China in return for silver and gold.

One of the most terrible of Samarkand's conquerors was *Tamerlane* or *Timur the Great Lame Man* (1370–1405). He was a Turkish warlord who gathered men from all over Asia into one vast army with which he sacked most of Asia's cities and towns. He chose Samarkand as his capital and brought in artists and workmen who were given the job of making it the most beautiful city in the world.

Fabulous treasures were taken to the city and magnificent palaces, mosques and tombs were built. One of the great surviving buildings of Timur's reign is the majestic Gur-Emir Mausoleum. Timur built it as a tomb for his grandson, the Mukhammed-Sultan, who died on a march to Turkey in 1403. The blue fluted dome of the tomb gleams amid the trees. Its walls are decorated with mosaics in different shades of blue, and the entrance is painted in white, green, blue, yellow, black and gold. The inside of the dome rivals the outside in its beauty and blue colour scheme. Beneath it lie the tombs of Timur, his sons and grandsons. Timur's skeleton rests under a great slab of dark-green jade behind a marble railing.

The graves of Timur and his family were untouched for over five hundred years until, in 1941, they were looked at by scientists. According to legend Timur was called the *'great lame man'*, and the watchers waited to see if the legend were true. When the last shovel of earth was removed from the grave a wooden coffin could be seen. It was in good condition even though the nails had rusted away. When the boards of the lid were lifted the skeleton of Timur was revealed for the first time and everyone crowded forward. There were no weapons or armour of any kind in the coffin. All eyes were now on the skeleton, quickly checking the bones of each leg. Sure enough, one leg was shorter than the other. Timur had really been lame and the ancient manuscripts had spoken the truth.

Timur's favourite wife, *Bibi-Khanym*, was not buried with her husband. For her Timur built what was then the largest mosque in the Islamic world. Of it was said that *'its dome would have been the only one in the universe, had not the sky been its replica, and its arch would have been unique had not the Milky Way been its match.'* Unfortunately, the mosque was almost completely destroyed by an earth-

50 quake several centuries ago, but the majestic ruins that still rise above the city like golden rocks manage to give a hint of its former glory.

It seems that the artists and workmen brought to Samarkand by Timur were fascinated by the vivid blueness of its sky. They took the colour and repeated it in every building so that it shines on the tall stems of the minarets and on the huge domes of the mosques. These unknown workmen created a rhapsody in blue which the world has admired for the last five hundred years.

Reginald Hutchinson

Understanding

Now you have read the passage answer the following questions. Choose the answer which you think best.

1 Samarkand has been called all of the following EXCEPT
   A gem of the world
   B spine of the earth
   C shining point of the globe
   D city of famous shadows

2 The Silk Road was used to transport all of the following EXCEPT
   A silver
   B silk
   C gold
   D cedarwood

3 Tamerlane was a warlord from
   A Samarkand
   B Timur
   C Asia
   D Turkey

4 The Gur-Emir Mausoleum was built as a tomb for
   A Alexander
   B Tamerlane
   C Mukhammed-Sultan
   D Ulugbek

5 The word 'fluted' most nearly means
   A wrinkled and lined
   B a fluttering movement
   C having rounded furrows or channels
   D to play or make sounds like a flute

6 Tamerlane's lameness was finally confirmed by the
   A lack of weapons or armour in the coffin
   B ancient manuscripts
   C good condition of the coffin
   D skeleton

7 Tamerlane's favourite wife was called
   A Gur-Emir
   B Bibi-Khanym
   C Ferghana
   D Shakki-Zindir

8 Which three of the following are dealt with at length in the passage?
   A invasion of India
   B tomb of Mukhammed-Sultan
   C murder of Ulugbek
   D exhumation of Tamerlane

9 The writer's attitude towards the buildings of Samarkand is
   A hostile
   B critical
   C favourable
   D neutral

10 The best title for this passage would be
   A Traveller's Tale
   B Rhapsody in Blue
   C Timur's City
   D A Stop on the Silk Road

Oral ideas

11 *Group project*   Talk over ways to present dramatically on tape, this ending to the verse play *Hassan* by James Elroy Flecker. How many Merchants and Jews will be needed, and what are the right voices for the solo speakers? What kind of background music will you choose? After rehearsals, listen to each group's version and then discuss which recording is best.

Epilogue to 'Hassan'

(AT THE GATE OF THE MOON, BAGHDAD)
THE MERCHANTS (*together*)
AWAY, for we are ready to a man!
  Our camels sniff the evening and are glad.
Lead on, O Master of the Caravan,
  Lead on the Merchant-Princes of Baghdad.

THE CHIEF DRAPER
Have we not Indian carpets dark as wine,
  Turbans and sashes, gowns and bows and veils,
And broideries of intricate design,
  And printed hangings in enormous bales?

THE CHIEF GROCER
We have rose-candy, we have spikenard,
  Mastic and terebinth and oil and spice,
And such sweet jams meticulously jarred
  As God's Own Prophet eats in Paradise.

THE PRINCIPAL JEWS
And we have manuscripts in peacock styles
  By Ali of Damascus: we have swords
Engraved with storks and apes and crocodiles,
  And heavy beaten necklaces for lords.

THE MASTER OF THE CARAVAN
But you are nothing but a lot of Jews.

PRINCIPAL JEW
Sirs, even dogs have daylight, and we pay.

MASTER OF THE CARAVAN
But who are ye in rags and rotten shoes,
  You dirty-bearded, blocking up the way?

ISHAK
We are the Pilgrims, master; we shall go
  Always a little further: it may be
Beyond that last blue mountain barred with snow,
  Across that angry or that glimmering sea,

White on a throne or guarded in a cave
  There lives a prophet who can understand
Why men were born: but surely we are brave,
  Who take the Golden Road to Samarkand.

THE CHIEF MERCHANT
We gnaw the nail of hurry. Master, away!

ONE OF THE WOMEN
  O turn your eyes to where your children stand.
Is not Bagdad the beautiful? O, stay!

MERCHANTS
We take the Golden Road to Samarkand.

HASSAN
Sweet to ride forth at evening from the wells,
  When shadows pass gigantic on the sand,
And softly through the silence beat the bells
  Along the Golden Road to Samarkand.

ISHAK
We travel not for trafficking alone;
  By hotter winds our fiery hearts are fanned:
For lust of knowing what should not be known,
  We take the Golden Road to Samarkand.

MASTER OF THE CARAVAN
Open the gate, O watchman of the night!

THE WATCHMAN
  Ho, travellers, I open. For what land
Leave you the dim-moon city of delight?

MERCHANTS (*with a shout*)
We take the Golden Road to Samarkand!
  (*The Caravan passes through the gate*)

Writing

12 Imagine you have joined the above caravan on its journey along the Golden Road to Samarkand. Tell of some of your adventures. It may help if you read the verses again.

13 The word for tea in central Asia is *Chai*, and in the *Chaikhana* (tearooms) it may be drunk with lemon, with jam, or with salt and butter. Imagine you have a visitor from central Asia. Explain for that visitor how you would make a good English pot of tea.

14 A well-known game for horsemen in the eastern part of Asia is called *Kyz-kuumai* (catch the girl). A horseman rides after a girl on horseback trying to overtake her. If he does he receives a kiss; if he fails he is slashed by her whip. Explain for a horseman from eastern Asia any showjumping event in which both sexes take part or an event of your own you have created.

15 The picture above shows the head and shoulders of Tamerlane as seen by the modern Russian sculptor Gerasimov. Look at it with care and then describe the face and the clothing, and the kind of person Gerasimov thought Tamerlane to be.

Activities and research

16 Prepare and write a short piece on any *one* of the following:

Alexander the Great	Jenghiz Khan
Omar Khayyam	Marco Polo
Baber	Akbar

Language in use

17 The words in the box have been taken from the passage on page 60. Match each with a phrase in the list below.

fabulous	mosque
pilgrimage	legend
mausoleum	mosaic
dome	manuscript
minaret	rhapsody

a a piece of ornamental work produced by fitting together small pieces of coloured stone or glass to form a pattern

b a large tomb raised over a grave of a famous or important person

c an expression of great praise and excitement

d a building in which Muslims worship

e nearly unbelievable

f a tall thin tower that forms part of a mosque

g a handwritten book of the time before printing was invented

h a journey to a place in which one has a respectful interest

i an old story about great deeds of ancient times

j a rounded top on a building

18 Punctuate this passage, rewriting it in your best handwriting:

central asia is at the heart of the old world, stretching from the bay of bengal to the eastern mediterranean it was once the cross road of routes leading from europe to india and from the middle east to china caravans of camels laden with furs and dates gold and salt started out from here travellers trudged west along the great silk route carrying in their staffs the larvae of the silkworm the key to the secret of chinese silk marco polo europes great wanderer trod this earth central asia was also the cross road of conquerors great military leaders like alexander of macedon jenghiz khan and tamerlane it was the meeting place of the great cultures of the west and east

Bathers Beware!

If you like swimming or paddling in the seas around our coast, you ought to know about creatures in the rock pools and shallow waters who do not want you there. They wish to be left in peace and will attack any intruder with results that can be quite painful. It is therefore wise to keep an eye open for any of the following when bathing in shallow coastal waters.

Jellyfish

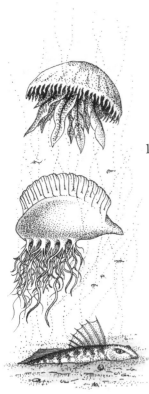

These have an umbrella-shaped, jelly-like, almost transparent body with tentacles underneath. They float freely in the sea but are poor swimmers. Strong winds sweep them ashore in large numbers.
10 Contact with jellyfish can cause the skin to itch and may even inflict the same kind of sting as that of the stinging nettle.

The Portuguese Man-of-War

This has often been mistaken for a plastic bag floating in the water. It is, in fact, a large poisonous jellyfish with long thread-like parts that hang beneath it. The umbrella-like head is harmless: the hanging tentacles do all the stinging.

The Sting Fish

A small, nasty, greyish looking fish found in the shallow waters of a sandy beach. It buries its body in the sand, leaving only the poisonous spines on its head sticking above ground. When trodden upon the stings from the spines can be very, very painful.

The Sea-Urchin

20 This can be found in warm waters stuck to rocks or on the sea bed. It has a spherical body protected by spikes and these cause problems for paddlers and swimmers. When trodden upon the spikes penetrate the skin and then break off. This brings about inflammation that can last many weeks.

The Sea-Anemone

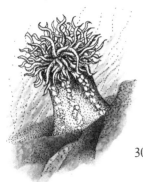

A simple sea animal that appears on sand and rocks in calm weather. It has a jelly-like body and beautiful 'leaves' that look just like the anemone flower grown in gardens. It is the brightly coloured 'leaves' that sting.

First Aid

Should you be stung by a jellyfish, and remember that Portuguese
30 Men-of-War are also jellyfish, these two things can be done:
i If you are near a kitchen then apply meat tenderiser to the spot: this will dissolve the stinging cells. Apply a cool dressing afterwards.

ii Should you be near a bathroom, get a wet razor and gently shave the affected skin until all bumps are removed.

Wounds received from a Sting Fish must be washed very carefully with salt water before the poison and the spines are sucked out. A hot compressed bandage soaked in manganese sulphate should then be applied every hour.

40   The spikes of Sea-Urchins can be sucked out and the infected area then bathed with an antiseptic.

Raymond Holloway

Comprehension and discussion

1 What does a Portuguese Man-of-War look like?
2 Explain the first aid you would apply if you were wounded by a Sting Fish.
3 Which of the stings mentioned is the most painful?
4 In one sentence, explain what would happen if you trod on the spike of a Sea-Urchin.
5 Why are jellyfish often swept ashore in large numbers?
6 What is the purpose behind applying a meat tenderiser to a jellyfish sting?
7 In one sentence, explain how you would deal with a jellyfish sting with a wet razor.

Summing up

8 Tell in not more than 50 of your own words what this passage is about.

Language in use

9 Give the meaning of:

coastal   transparent   tentacles
intruder

10 Use in sentences:

inflict   spherical   inflammation
compressed

11 Which of these words most nearly means the same as *intruder*, as it is used in the passage?

stranger   foreigner   alien
outsider   newcomer

12 Find a word that means the opposite to *transparent*.
13 Why is *Sting Fish* spelt with capital letters?
14 Write down five words that like *antiseptic* begin with *anti*. What does the prefix *anti* mean?
15 The plural of *Portuguese Man-of-War* is *Portuguese Men-of-War*. What is the plural of the following:

spoonful   mosquito   man-in-charge
passer-by   commander-in-chief

Writing

16 Here are some words about the seashore. Use as many of them as possible in a poem or short piece of writing.

shingle	waves	tide
buoy	rocks	flotsam
coves	sandbank	caves
shells	groyne	cliffs
breakwater	jetty	spray
limpets	surf	jetsam
gulls	seaweed	

17 Choose a seaside place you know or have seen on television. Try to imagine the sounds and the smells and anything that reminds you of the place. Write down your ideas. Look through them and try to add one or two small word pictures, e.g. *gulls screaming like hysterical children*. Now write a vivid account of your seaside place.
18 Imagine that you are skin-diving and that you meet an octopus or some other dangerous sea creature. Describe your experiences as vividly as you can.

5 Personal expression

Contents

Shame

Once, when I was about nine my father lost his job and couldn't get another one. We were evicted from our house and sent to live in the poor ward of a local hospital. This ward contained about a hundred beds divided from each other by grey blankets hung on ropes. It was full of women and children. No fathers were allowed. Mine slept in the park and got shaved in the public lavatory every day. I was terribly ashamed of living in the hospital. I had always thought poor old loonies went there, not ordinary people like us. Every afternoon
10 I used to sneak the long way round coming from school so nobody would see where I lived. I know it shouldn't have mattered to me but it did. Anyway one day this girl in my class, Jean Meredith, followed me home. I didn't see her but next day everyone in my class knew I lived in the hospital. I tried to pretend I didn't care but just a few odd remarks to the girl sitting next to me about being careful what she caught really hurt. I couldn't wait for the day to end and I thought I would never go back to that school again even if I had to play truant every day.

That afternoon we had English and we were reading a play. Our class teacher, Miss Sansom, picked people to go to the front of the
20 class and act it. She told me to read Dick Whittington. The part of the play we did that afternoon was where he was on the road to London in his rags. He feels hopeless and decides to give up the idea of going to London, and return home. I suppose I read it with feeling because I was poor too and life was looking pretty hopeless for me. When Miss Sansom rang the classroom bell, pretending to be the bells of London and one of the boys said, 'Turn again, Whittington, Lord Mayor of London', I was overcome with joy. It seemed like it was really me it was happening to. Then the lesson finished and I was just me again, still humiliated. Before she started the next lesson
30 Miss Sansom held her hand up for silence. 'Lesley,' she said. 'Have you ever thought of being an actress when you grow up? I think you'd be a very good one.' Everybody looked at me. I went bright red. I thought it was like Dick Whittington hearing the bells, but this time it really was for me. What she said didn't change anything: I still had to go home to the hospital. But that day and many days after I walked home with a wonderful feeling inside me.

Lesley Davies

Comprehension and discussion

1 What does 'evicted' mean in the second sentence?

2 Why were they evicted from their home?

3 Why was the large ward divided up by blankets hanging on ropes?

4 What did Lesley do so that the other pupils would not know where she lived?

5 What did Jean Meredith do and what did she say that hurt Lesley so much?

6 Why did Lesley pretend that she did not care? How do we know that in fact she really did care?

7 Why did she go bright red?

8 Explain how she felt about reading the part in the play and why her feelings changed from shame to joy.

9 Is there anything to be ashamed of in being poor? Why do some people look down on other people who are not as well off as they are?

10 Do you think it right that the families should have been separated and made to live in those conditions?

Writing

11 Write out a conversation that might have taken place between Lesley Davies and some of her friends in which they discuss this incident. During the conversation Jean Meredith comes along.

12 Describe someone you know who is always showing off about what he or she has.

13 Describe fully a situation in which you were very embarrassed or deeply hurt.

Oral ideas

14 Consider arguments that break out between members of your class. Why do some people seem to enjoy making hurting remarks about others? What weapons do they often use to hurt them?

No Man's Land

This incident comes from a story about the Spanish Civil War. Will and Griff are two British boys who join in the war. No man's land is the territory between the two opposing armies.

In the dark, north, south, east and west wore the same featureless mask. The stars were overclouded, and anyway neither Will nor Griff could read the stars.

The thought of crawling into a trench and finding not their friends but a scowling enemy, made Will stop. 'We need to take our bearings.'

Instinctively, they crouched down and at the very same moment the hill halfway up the sky burst into flame. An explosion raised the lid of darkness.

10 Smaller explosions burst on the heels of the first.

There was a second of silence before the entire battle-front unleashed its armoury. Somehow the blackness made things worse. Distance closed in. Between a machine-gun barrel and the victim was sightlessness — no matter that in daylight you couldn't see the bullets either.

Head down, smelling the bitter winter earth, hands clamped over ears. A bullet smashed stone close by. Another ricocheted off rocks to the left or right.

Will raised his eyes as the intensity of the gunfire wavered — and 20 got the very worst shock of his life. His gaze fell on another face.

The enemy soldier lay belly down, pointing in the direction of his own trenches as Will and Griff were pointing at theirs. He was as terrified as Will — and as young: wan faced, pop-eyed, immovable as though his limbs had been driven into the ground with wooden stakes.

If he was armed, there was no sign of it. At the sight of two of the enemy, he rolled sideways like a rabbit springing from the hand about to descend upon its neck.

Will said, 'Please!' It was all he could think of: please — don't do 30 anything, don't shoot, don't run. But Griff cut words. This was the closest bang, the closest bullet and it drowned Will's anguished 'No, Griff!'

Too late. The bullet was straight. The enemy turned half in a circle. His hand was raised as if to some invisible support, some arm held out to him in the last flash of his living mind.

His pop-eyed face fell back before the rest of him.

'There was no need!'

''Im or us.'

'He'd no gun.'

40 'Beggar that!'

Will was across the body. 'If he's only wounded — '

'Forget 'im. 'E's dead.'

The young Spaniard lay as only the dead lie. Yet Will would not let him go. Feebly, he bent over him, willing breath back into him.

'Sorry, sorry. . .'

He no longer heard the flying bullets. He did not care whether they struck him. The pop eyes were in his head. He could see nothing but them.

50 One life. Sixteen years of caring and loving and feeding, of laughing and crying and running and talking — turned, in a single moment, to cold flesh.

James Watson
The Freedom Tree

Comprehension and discussion

1 What does the first sentence emphasise about the boys' situation?
2 Why do neither Will nor the Spanish boy move when they see each other?
3 Describe carefully Will's feelings from the moment he saw the boy to the end of the passage. Quote from the passage to support what you say.
4 Why were Griff's feelings different from those of Will?
5 How do we know that Will and Griff were only teenagers?
6 How are the wastefulness and cruelty of war emphasised at the end of the passage?

Language in use

7 Consider carefully *each* of the following adjectives and say briefly why you think it applies or does not apply first to Will and then to Griff:

cowardly   daring   cruel   sensitive

8 Explain what the following words or expressions mean in the passage and say what they add to the description or to your understanding of the incident:

unleashed its armoury (line 12)
wan faced (line 23)
pop-eyed (line 23)
willing breath into him (line 44)

Writing

9 Write two paragraphs describing the feelings and thoughts of Will and Griff while the shells were exploding.
10 Write out the conversation that could have taken place between Will and Griff after they had reached safety.
11 Imagine that years later Will and Griff, now married with families, went to Spain on holiday and met a Spanish couple who turned out to be the parents of the dead boy. Describe the meeting between them.
12 Describe a situation in which you felt great fear.

Oral ideas

13 What is a civil war? Give examples. Should foreigners stay out of them?
14 Do you agree with Griff when he said "Im or us'?
15 Why do war films and films which have so much killing and fighting in them seem so popular?
16 Arrange a debate on violence on television and videos.

Her First Pop Concert

The recent and abrupt demand from my 13-year-old daughter that she should be allowed to attend her first pop concert focussed my attention on the fact that she was no longer a child. Changes had obviously taken place in her over the previous eight months that I had missed.

How, I asked, when the air had cleared a little and parental opposition to the idea of a pop concert had waned, did she and a friend intend to get to and from Wembley Arena, a round journey of some considerable distance? Her reply was terse and to the point.
10 'You will take us,' she said.

An horrific vision of drug pushers besieging thousands of vulnerable youngsters locked into music-crazed hysteria filled my mind. With great reluctance I sent off for the tickets, nursing the secret hope that they would be sold out before my cheque arrived. My daughter had been 13 last summer. Then pop music played no part in her life. She would listen to Radio 3 while wrestling with her homework in her bedroom.

Almost overnight the dial on the portable stereo flipped to Capital Radio and the bedroom was filled with the convulsive throb of pop
20 music. A weekly pop magazine, tagged I later discovered on to my newspaper account, was suddenly in evidence. Within days posters of Duran Duran covered every inch of available wall space. No matter, I thought. Academic work fills vast amounts of my daughter's time and if pop music helps her to relax, then so be it.

With her growing awareness of pop music came a growing emphasis on, and concern for, clothes; jeans and baggy jumpers, fashionable boots and lace blouses, were mixed together and worn with panache. The way she wore her long blonde hair (currently about to become copper coloured) also began to preoccupy her.
30 Should it be piled on top or pulled to the side and twisted into a tight roll. Experimentation with make-up began, the results often producing comic effects. Parental laughter brought forth histrionic responses as she tested the limits of our authority.

Eventually the tickets for Duran Duran's last appearance of their current tour arrived. *The Times* pop music writer allayed my more extreme fears. No, he said, there would not be any nastiness at the concert. The group's following was mostly young and innocent. It would be, he said, the equivalent of a Cliff Richard concert of 20 years ago.
40 He was right. The journey by tube to Wembley with youngsters on all sides bubbling with energy and excitement was an amazing experience. A carnival atmosphere filled the streets to the arena. Girls dressed in dazzling and improvised fashions of black and silver rubbed shoulders with boys decked out in sleek-cut denim, their hair (both sexes) flecked with blonde streaks, and make-up (both sexes again) carefully and seriously applied. No punks, no aggression, no trouble.

Late that evening as the concert drew to a close hundreds of parents crowded the pavement at Wembley. The level of noise coming from the arena was astonishing. Youngsters who left early to catch trains released great gulps of sound as they pushed out through the swing doors. Then it was over. Thousands of make-up smudged kids, still moving and heaving to the strange rhythms found in the arena, poured out. Anxious parents stretched their necks and waved newspapers in an effort to make themselves seen. Chatter and excitement filled the air. Posters and programmes were clutched in young hands made sore from clapping. Largesse was everywhere. A group of charity collectors, rattling boxes, swept down among the parents who dipped deep into their own pockets. Volvos and Rovers purred into life, the drivers looking very middle class and staid in comparison to their exuberant passengers. I suddenly felt so middle-aged and out of touch.

Michael Young
The Times

Comprehension and discussion

1 When Michael Young's daughter asked to be allowed to go to the pop concert what was his first reply?

2 What did her request make him realise?

3 Why did he not want her to go?

4 What did he secretly hope for when he sent for the tickets? Give your opinion of this.

5 Make a list of the ways in which he saw his daughter had changed.

6 Why did his daughter try so many different types of hair styles and clothes? Was she vain?

7 Describe what happened when his daughter tried to use make-up.

8 What did she have to rely on her father to do in arranging the outing?

9 How was he reassured that there would be no trouble at the concert?

10 What were the feelings of the parents waiting outside Wembley? How did they contrast with the feelings of the youngsters coming out?

11 Write a brief description of the sort of parent Michael Young seems to be and support your opinions with reference to the passage.

Language in use

12 Which words or expressions best describe the air of excitement before the concert?

13 Which two words in the next to the last sentence are opposite in meaning? What do they emphasise?

14 Use a dictionary and then say what the following mean in the passage:

terse convulsion worn with panache histrionic testing the limits of our will carnival atmosphere largesse improvised fashions

Writing

15 Write out a conversation between you and your friends in which you discuss how you are going to approach your parents to be allowed to go on a similar outing.

16 Describe your feelings when you took part in a similar situation full of excitement.

17 Do you think that Michael Young's attitude would have been the same if it had been his son asking to go to the concert or to a football match? Develop your ideas on this.

Oral ideas

18 Why do girls of this age want to wear make-up when they have fresh, young skins? Is there any equivalent show that boys make?

19 Discuss with people of an older generation what pop concerts were like in their day (e.g. Beatles, Cliff Richard, Elvis Presley) and write a short article comparing them with modern ones.

Extracts from the Diary of Adrian Mole

Wednesday March 11th

Dragged myself to school after doing paper round and housework. My mother wouldn't give me a note excusing me from Games so I left my PE kit at home. I just couldn't face running about in the cold wind.

That sadist Mr Jones made me run all the way home to fetch my PE kit. The dog must have followed me out of the house because when I got to the school gate it was there before me. I tried to shut the dog out but it squeezed through the railings and followed me into the playground. I ran into the changing rooms and left the dog outside but I could hear its loud bark echoing around the school. I tried to sneak into the playing fields but the dog saw me and followed behind, then it saw the football and joined in the lesson! The dog is dead good at football, even Mr Jones was laughing until the dog punctured the ball.

Mr Scruton, the pop-eyed headmaster, saw everything from his window. He ordered me to take the dog home. I told him I would miss my sitting for school dinners but he said it would teach me not to bring pets to school.

Mrs Leech, the kitchen supervisor, did a very kind thing. She put my curry and rice, spotted dick and custard into the oven to keep warm. Mrs Leech doesn't like Mr Scruton so she gave me a large marrow-bone to take home for the dog.

Wednesday April 1st

ALL FOOLS' DAY

Nigel rang up this morning and pretended he was an undertaker and asked when he was to pick up the body. My father answered the phone. Honestly. He has got no sense of humour.

I had a good laugh telling girls that their petticoats were showing when they weren't. Barry Kent brought a packet of itching powder into the Art lesson, he put some down Ms Fossington-Gore's flying boots. She is another one without any sense of humour. Barry Kent put some down my back. It wasn't funny. I had to go to the matron and have it removed.

The house is looking extremely squalid because my father is not doing any housework. The dog is pining for my mother.

I was born exactly thirteen years and three hundred and sixty-four days ago.

Wednesday April 15th

Went to the youth club with Nigel. It was dead good. We played ping-pong until the balls cracked. Then we had a go on the football table. I beat Nigel fifty goals to thirteen. Nigel went into a sulk and said that he only lost because his goalkeeper's legs were stuck on with Sellotape but he was wrong. It was my superior skill that did it.

A gang of punks passed unkind comments about my flared trousers but Rick Lemon, the youth leader, stepped in and led a discussion on personal taste. We all agreed it should be up to the individual to dress how he or she likes. All the same I think I will ask my father if I can have a new pair of trousers. Not many fourteen-year-olds wear flared trousers today, and I don't wish to be conspicuous.

Barry Kent tried to get in the fire-doors to avoid paying his five-pence subs. But Rick Lemon pushed him back outside into the rain. I was very pleased. I owe Barry Kent two pounds' menaces money.

Thursday May 21st

Barry Kent duffed me up in the cloakroom today. He hung me on one of the coathooks. He called me a 'coppers' nark' and other things too bad to write down. My grandma found out about the menacing (my father didn't want her to know on account of her diabetes). She listened to it all then she put her hat on, thinned her lips and went out. She was gone one hour and seven minutes, she came in, took her coat off, fluffed her hair out, took £27.18 from the anti-mugger belt round her waist. She said, 'He won't bother you again, Adrian, but if he does, let me know.' Then she got the tea ready. Pilchards, tomatoes and ginger cake. I bought her a box of diabetic chocolates from the chemist's as a token of my esteem.

Friday May 22nd

It is all round the school that an old lady of seventy-six frightened Barry Kent and his dad into returning my menaces money. Barry Kent daren't show his face. His gang are electing a new leader.

Wednesday October 21st

Hobbled to school. All the teachers were wearing their best clothes because it is Parents' Evening tonight. My father got cleaned up and put his best suit on. He looked OK, Thank God! Nobody could tell he was unemployed. My teachers all told him that I was a credit to the school.

Barry Kent's father was looking as sick as a pig. Ha! Ha! Ha!

Sue Townsend
The Secret Diary of Adrian Mole Aged 13¾

Comprehension and discussion

1 How did his trick of deliberately forgetting his PE kit backfire on him?
2 Describe the tricks that were played on the 1st of April. What do they tell us about his sense of humour?
3 When they discussed fashions in clothes what decision did the members of the youth club arrive at? Do you think it was an honest decision as far as Adrian was concerned?
4 Describe Barry Kent's activities and the type of lad he is.
5 Write three or four lines describing Adrian's grandmother.
6 Say how Adrian uses his diary to get his own back on people he does not like.
7 On the evidence of these extracts, give as full a character description of Adrian as you can. Pay attention to those parts where he shows aspects of his character without intending to do so.

Language in use

8 What does Adrian mean when he says 'dead good', 'duffed me up'. What type of English is this? Should it be used in a diary?

9 What do the following mean in the passage?

squalid   flared   menaces

10 When Adrian says his grandmother 'thinned her lips' what does he mean? What other word do we often use for this action?

Writing

11 Imagine you are Mr Jones and you also keep a diary. Write an extract for 11th of March.
12 Write extracts of your own diary for:
a 1st of April
b a few days before a school disco and the day after
c a day when something very unusual happened at school
13 Why do people like reading other people's diaries?
14 If you found a diary belonging to:
a a teacher you like,
b a teacher you do not like,
c a close friend,
would you read them? Give reasons for your answer.
15 Make up a short story about finding somebody else's diary.

Personal Letters

Two personal letters

Hilde Coppi was arrested by the Nazis in September 1942, together with her husband Hans, because they belonged to a resistance group in Germany. In prison she gave birth to a son, Hans. One month later her husband was executed. When her son was eight months old, Hilde was executed. She was 34 years old.

Hilde wrote this letter on her last day:

5 August 1943

My Mother, my dearly beloved Mama,

Now the time has almost come when we must say farewell for ever. The hardest part, the separation from my little Hans, is behind me. How happy he made me! I know that he will be well taken care of in your loyal, dear maternal hands, and for my sake, Mama — promise me — remain brave. I know that you feel as though your heart must break; but take yourself firmly in hand, very firmly. You will succeed, as you always have, in coping with the severest difficulties, won't you, Mama? The thought of you and of the deep
10 sorrow that I must inflict upon you is the most unbearable of all — the thought that I must leave you alone at that time of life when you need me most! Will you ever, ever be able to forgive me? As a child, you know, when I used to lie awake so long, I was always animated by one thought — to be allowed to die before you. And later, I had a single wish that constantly accompanied me, consciously and unconsciously: I did not want to die without having brought a child into the world. So you see, both of these great desires, and thereby my life, have attained fulfilment. Now I am going to join my big Hans. Little Hans has — so I hope — inherited
20 the best in both of us. And when you press him to your heart, your child will always be with you, much closer than I can ever be to you. Little Hans — this is what I wish — will become hardy and strong, with an open, warm, helpful heart and his father's thoroughly decent character. We love each other very, very much. Love guided our actions . . .

My mother, my one and only good mother and my little Hans, all my love is always with you; be brave, as I am determined also to be.

Always,
Your daughter Hilde

14 Mersey Ave
Market Bosworth
Leics.

26th June

Dear Aunty Trudie,

Thank you for the beautiful writing set you sent me for my birthday. My old one had just ran out when I got the parcel. The set you sent me is the most beautiful one that I've ever seen.

I had a lovely birthday. I got a lot of money so I've decided to save up for a radio. I also got two skirts and a pair of shoes.

Mum, Dad, the baby, the dog and cat send their love
from your loving niece,
Elizabeth

A thank-you letter

Advice from the Post Office on letter writing

Can you make a list of all the people who would enjoy getting a letter from you? Aunts and uncles? Grandparents? Friends who have moved away? Special private friends?

What do they want to hear from you? What makes a good letter?

Well, nobody can make any rules about how you write to a close friend. How you set out that letter and what you say is a matter between the two of you. You should write that letter in the same way as you would talk to that person. But you won't want to bore them.

So remember: when you write to a friend or a member of the family, write as though you were talking to them.

10

Getting organised

Even though we have said that there are no rules about letters that you send to a close friend, there are ways of making a letter easier and more interesting for that friend to receive.

So, before you start your letter, plan what you want to say, and decide what order you will put it all in.

For example:

What's the first thing you want to say to your friend?

What news have you got to share (since you last wrote or since you last saw your friend)?

20 What is the most sensible order to tell the news in?

What points (if any) have you got to answer from your friend's last letter?

What do you want to ask your friend about?

Have you any plans to make for the future? (Perhaps you have some arrangements to make about a meeting.)

For each topic or section of your letter, start a new paragraph.

Make sure you explain anything your friend may be unsure about.

Write clearly and neatly so that your friend will have no trouble reading the letter.

30 Leave a margin round the page.

Do read through what you have written. Make sure you have not missed anything out, and that your letter says what you want it to say.

How does your letter get there?

Every day, 35 million letters are posted. Yes, 35 million. Imagine having to sort them!

That's why it's important that each letter is addressed correctly and clearly.

After a letter has been collected from a letter box, it is taken to the nearest post office for sorting. In busy post offices, it passes

40 through several machines which sort the letters into different sizes, stack them all the same way up (with the addresses at the front), check they are stamped, separate first and second class letters and then stamp them all with a postmark.

In mechanised sorting offices a person sits at a machine which has a keyboard a bit like a typewriter. This person copies the postcode of the address the letter is being sent to on to the keyboard. The machine then prints the postcode in blue phosphor dots on the envelope.

From now on, other machines can 'read' these dots, and so the

50 letter can be sorted automatically at each stage of its journey.

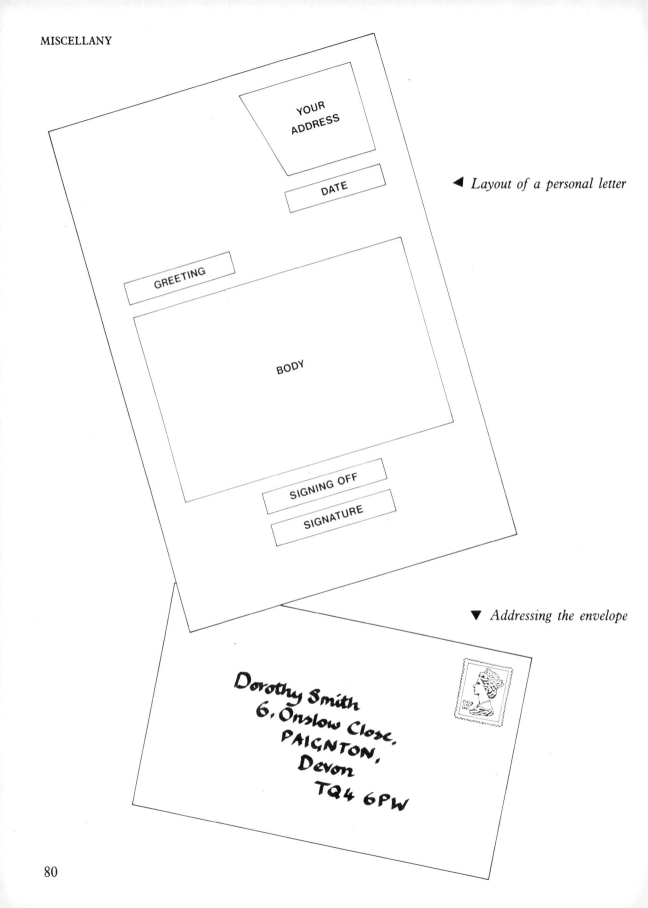

YOUR
ADDRESS

DATE

◀ *Layout of a personal letter*

GREETING

BODY

SIGNING OFF

SIGNATURE

▼ *Addressing the envelope*

Dorothy Smith
6, Onslow Close,
PAIGNTON,
Devon
TQ4 6PW

Addressing the envelope

Remember these points when addressing a letter:

If the address begins too high up, the postmark may hide part of it. The top line should be at least 40 mm from the top of the envelope.

If you start the address too low down, you may not be able to fit it all on the envelope.

Just occasionally a letter may have to be returned to the person who sent it. To help the Post Office, put your own name and address on the back of the envelope, at the top.

60 Write the post town (the town from which your letter will be delivered) in BLOCK CAPITALS. It is not always necessary to include the county. If it is included, it should not be in capitals.

The postcode should be written clearly as the last line of the address.

If you are unsure about your own correct address, or postcode, ask your parents, or check at your local post office.

Comprehension and discussion

1 Why does the Post Office advise us to put our address on the back of the envelope? Do you agree with their advice? Why do you think many people do not follow it?

2 Why can there be no rules concerning letters sent to close friends?

3 Although there are no rules, what good practices should you follow? Make a list of them.

4 Do you think that such letters as the first example, which is very personal, should be published for other people to read?

5 Why does the Post Office regard the postcode as a very important part of an address?

6 Describe what happens to a letter from the time it is posted to its being delivered.

7 If a personal letter is a conversation between you and your friend, what parts of the conversation are missing?

Writing

8 Write personal letters using the information as follows:

a You met someone on holiday and you would like to see that person again.

b An invitation to a close friend to a birthday party.

c A pop concert/football game is about to take place and you would like to go to it. However, tickets are scarce. You hear that a cousin of yours might have some. Write a letter asking for tickets.

d You have fallen out with a close friend and you want to make it up.

e While on holiday you run out of money and write an emergency letter home asking for more.

6 Argument

Contents

A Greek Story

This story was part of an advertisement for Greek holidays. Read it with care and then answer the questions that follow.

Clive and his wife were driving in southern Crete, trying to find their way to a particular mountain village. Hopelessly lost, they stopped and asked a Cretan the way. Typically he spoke some English.

'Straight up that road,' he said. 'It is a bad road but you can make it.' They drove along the road for a few miles until they found the way blocked by a mountain of gravel. An old man standing on the gravel made circular motions with his hand, and Clive switched off the engine. The old man then leaped into a bulldozer and proceeded to carve a path through the gravel. Five minutes later he smilingly
10 waved them through a billowing cloud of dust.

Driving on a few miles more our adventurers once again found themselves hopelessly lost and decided to call it a day. Pulling in at the first small taverna in the next village they came to, they wearily slumped into chairs at the solitary table on a small terrace in front of the taverna, and a waiter appeared.

'Two Greek coffees, please,' said Clive, and the waiter nodded and trotted off into the dim interior. Over coffee, Clive and his wife got down to the national Greek pastime of just sitting and watching the world go by, joined we might add, by the friendly waiter.
20 A little later, Clive ordered two Rakis (a potent Greek spirit), and being a generous soul bought the waiter a drink as well. Time rolled pleasantly on, as it usually does in Greece, and eventually Clive asked the waiter for the bill. 'There is no charge,' he said.

'Oh,' said Clive, 'that's very kind of you — do you own this taverna?' 'No,' said the Greek, poker faced, 'and this isn't a taverna, it's my house.'

Comprehension and discussion

1 In which country did Clive's story take place?

2 When Clive stopped to ask the way, how do we know that the person was telling the truth?

3 How did the old man show that he wanted to stop the engine of Clive's car?

4 What is a taverna? What clues are there in the story?

5 Tell, in your own words, what the writer thinks is the Greek national pastime.

6 The Greek people are said to be both friendly and generous. How does the story show this?

7 What is the point Clive's story is trying to make?

8 Give a title (but not 'Clive's Story') for this passage.

Summing up

9 Tell, in not more than 30 of your own words, what this story is about.

Language in use

10 Use a dictionary to find and write out the meaning of:

potent   slumped   terrace   pastime

11 Use in sentences:

hopelessly   typically   billowing
eventually

12 Change to adjectives:

mountain   dust   Greece   world
kind   soul

13 Take these words from the story and place them in alphabetical order:

Clive   Cretan   can   circular
carve   cloud   call   chairs
charge   coffees

14 *Mono* is the Greek prefix for *one*. Work out the meaning of:

monocle   monorail   monoplane
monotone   monologue   monopoly
monomania

15 Find a word which is the antonym of *interior*.

16 Say which of the following are sentences and which are phrases:

a   Up by the mountain of gravel
b   The waiter said nothing
c   All evening long
d   The Rakis were potent
e   Next to the taverna
f   Clive was lost
g   Dust billows
h   As hot as fire
i   Into the village they went
j   Can I have the bill, please?

17 Turn these phrases into sentences by making suitable additions:

a   In very olden times there lived in Greece . . . .
b   Athena, after whom the city of Athens was named, ...

. . . .
c   Zeus, the ruler of the gods,

. . . .
d   At the gate of the sun-god's palace

. . . .
e   In spite of his wounds the Greek warrior . . . .
f   Bright clothing that shone like gold

. . . .
g   Arachne was known throughout the land . . . .

18 Punctuate this passage, rewriting it in your best handwriting:

perseus do you know me she asked indeed i do said perseus you are the great goddess athena well said athena we gods are going to help you first look at this and she showed him the image of a head the face was very beautiful but cruel cold and unhappy instead of hair it had curling ringlets of snakes all round that is the gorgon medusa athena said but if you look at the real face you will be turned to stone then how can i get the head asked perseus take this shield and she gave him a shield smooth and shining like a mirror and when you come to medusa keep your back to her and look at her image in the shield so as to strike back over your shoulder then cut her head off and put it in this bag and she gave him a large leather bag be careful to leave her sisters alone for they are immortal medusa alone is mortal and she can be killed

Activities and research

19 Write a script for a radio dramatisation of the story of 'Daedalus and Icarus'. Check the story first.

20 Look up the name *Homer* in any encyclopaedia or reference book. Make notes of the information given, and then in your own words write an account of what you have learned about this man.

21 Research, write and illustrate a description of a holiday on any of the following Greek islands:

Zante   Ios   Aegina   Poros
Hydra   Spetse   Mykonos   Corfu

22 The following words come from Greek myths and legends. Use a dictionary or other reference book to explain the meaning of each one.

acanthus   acropolis   ambrosia
bacchanalian   centaur   chimera
labyrinth   nectar   oracle
quagmire   sirens   zephyr

Writing

23 Think of the wreck of an ancient Greek ship laden with statues, pottery and treasure, lying in clear blue water at the foot of a steep cliff. Write a story in which that ship plays a part.

24 Which holiday or event will you remember in twenty years' time? Give a detailed account of what made it so memorable.

25 Study the picture above. How much can you see? Write it all down as if you had been watching the scene and wanted to tell someone about it.

Mother Nature and her last will BY ART BUCHWALD

The other night I was home reading a book when I received a telephone call that Mother Nature was dying. I dressed hurriedly and rushed over to the hospital. . . . I searched out the doctors who were in another room having a heated argument as to how to save her. Each doctor seemed to have a different remedy.

One doctor said: 'We have to get her some fresh air. She can't breathe. We'll have to turn off the power plant because of the smoke.'

'Gentlemen,' another doctor said, 'I don't believe it's the air that is hurting her as much as the water. We have to find some water that's drinkable. Strong measures must be taken immediately against polluting hospital water.'

The director said: 'Where would we get the money to support the hospital if we closed down the factories because they're polluting the streams?'

'We'd also have to give up detergents,' a doctor added, 'and we can't have a clean hospital if you give up detergents.'

'Isn't anybody going to do anything?' I shouted.

They saw me for the first time, and one of the doctors said angrily, 'We're sorry, this is a medical conference for professionals only. Would you kindly leave.'

I walked out and down the hall. Suddenly I saw a closed room, which had the name MOTHER NATURE hand-printed on the door. Underneath it, in large red letters, was another sign: NO VISITORS.

No one was in the hall, so I opened the door. There was Mother Nature propped up on pillows. She looked old and tired and haggard. . . . But she seemed glad to see someone and smiled weakly.

'Hi Ma,' I said. 'You're looking swell.'

'You wouldn't kid a very sick lady, would you?' she said, gasping.

'No, I'm not kidding. You look wonderful. I've just been talking to the doctors, and they say they'll have you on your feet in no time.'

'Those quacks don't know anything,' she said. '. . . I think I've had it this time.'

'It's never been this bad,' she said and then started having a coughing fit. 'This time the Grim Reaper's coming to get me.'

'But if you go, we'll all have to go, Ma,' I cried. 'You have to hold on. Please, Ma.'

'I kept complaining of pain,' she whispered, 'but no one would pay attention to me. I said, "If you keep doing what you're doing, I'm going to die." But everyone said, "Ma, you'll never die." Why didn't they listen to me?'

'We're listening now, Ma. We're listening. We have the best doctors in the world. They're out there now, and they have a plan.'

'I guess the real thing that hurts,' she said, 'is that my will won't be worth anything now. I left every person in the world clear water, pure air, green fields, brilliant sunsets and blue skies. It wasn't much, but it was everything I had.'□

© 1983, *Los Angeles Times Syndicate*

Comprehension and discussion

1 Copy out three words from this article that show it was written by an American.

2 Tell in your own words the remedies suggested by the doctors as cures for Mother Nature.

3 What reasons were given for not using the remedies?

4 Why was the writer noticed by the doctors?

5 Why was he asked to leave the conference room?

6 How had Mother Nature changed in ten years?

7 Who is the Grim Reaper?

8 Explain 'But if you go, we'll all have to go, Ma'.

9 Tell in your own words why Mother Nature thought her will would now be useless.

Writing

10 Write opening paragraphs in the style of Art Buchwald for newspaper articles about:
a cigarette smoking, and
b alcohol abuse.

11 Write an article about children's television programmes for a teenage magazine.

12 Write an article for a school magazine arguing *for* and *against* the wearing of school uniform.

13 'Sport is not a very important part of life and it is being taken far too seriously.' Give your views in about 200 words.

14 In *Cosmic Poem*, the poet John Heath-Stubbs said:
Outer Space can wait its turn:
The human being's my concern.
What are your feelings about the exploration of outer space?

Oral ideas

15 *Individual* Bring to school a small part of nature — a stone, a shell, some soil, sand or gravel, a stuffed animal or fish, flowers, leaves etc. Use it first to give a short talk and then as the starting point for a class discussion.

Language in use

16 Work in pairs or small groups. Collect from magazines as many full page advertisements as possible for each of the following products:

food   cosmetics   detergents   cars

Use them to answer these questions:

a Choose one advertisement for each group of products. Cross out every adjective. Look at what is left. What effect did the adjectives have? Why were so many adjectives used? Tell in a paragraph or two about the use of adjectives in advertising.

b Find and copy out five examples of simile and five of metaphor in the advertisements.

c Write down as many words as you can that belong to each group of products, e.g. *fresh* and *clean* for toothpaste, *delicious*, *fresh* and *crisp* for foods, and *safe* and *sure* for soaps, detergents and deodorants. Write a short report on the words used to advertise food, cosmetics, detergents and cars.

d Here is a list of verbs used quite often in advertising:

buy	give	taste
go	look	feel
start	take	make
use	choose	come

Copy them out and by the side of each one show the number of times they appear in your advertisements. Add other verbs that you find are often used. Write a short report on the use of verbs in advertisements and what those verbs are telling the reader to do.

e Look at the pictures in your advertisements and then answer the following questions:

  i What is it about each picture that attracted your attention?

  ii Does any picture seem to be more important than the words of the advertisement?

  iii If there are men, women or children in any of the pictures can you say why they are there?

  iv What effect is the advertiser trying to achieve with each of the pictures?

  v At whom are the pictures aimed?

f Find an advertisement that you consider good and one you feel is bad. Say why you have made this choice.

g Make a report to the class in session of what you have discovered from this survey.

Activities and research

17 Find out what you can about each of the following:

acid rain
animals that are becoming extinct
the danger of nuclear power plants
the dumping of radioactive waste
the disappearance of the world's rain forests

When you have collected enough information write an article about the pollution and destruction of our natural world.

18 Design a poster/advertisement campaign of your own for any issue about which you feel strongly.

19 When Art Buchwald writes about nature as if it were a person, he is using a figure of speech known as *personification*. We do this in daily life, for example, when we call our car 'she' and even give 'her' a feminine name. A similar example to *Mother Nature* is *Ol' Man River*, a personification for the Mississippi river. Use your library to find and record ten other examples of personification.

Two Generations of Progress

Have you ever stopped to think of the great debt you owe your parents and grandparents?

Within their lifetimes they have worked to increase your life expectancy by nearly 50 per cent, to cut the working day by a third, and to more than double the output per person.

Your parents and grandparents have given you a healthier world than the one they entered. No longer must you fear epidemics of smallpox, measles, diphtheria, scarlet fever, mumps or typhus. Today no one hears of tuberculosis and the awful infantile paralysis is no longer with us.

These are the people who lived through one of the greatest economic depressions in history. They knew what it was to be poor, what it was to be hungry, and what it was to be cold. The experience made them determined that those who came after would have a better life, with food to eat, milk to drink, vitamins to nourish, warm homes, better schools and greater opportunities to succeed. Their determination has made you the tallest, healthiest and best educated generation to inhabit this country.

Your parents and grandparents were materialistic, and because of this you will work fewer hours, learn more, have more leisure, travel to more distant places, and have more chances to follow your life's ambition.

These also were the people who fought or suffered man's most gruesome war: the Second World War killed twenty million Russians and fifteen million elsewhere. They are the people who helped smash the mailed fist of Hitler and lift his reign of terror from the Jews. When that war was over they had the compassion to spend vast sums of money to help their former enemies rebuild their countries, and the sense to start the United Nations.

Your parents and grandparents had their failures. They did not find an alternative to war or to racial hatred. It will be for you to find those answers so that all men may follow their lives, hopes and ambitions without the threat of force. Earth will then no longer need police to enforce the laws, nor armies to prevent one country trespassing against another.

These two generations made more progress than any other two in history, and don't you forget it.

Roy Harris

Comprehension and discussion

1 Which generation is the writer trying to persuade?
2 Tell in your own words how health has improved during the last two generations.
3 Why was there a determination to see that after the Depression future generations would have a better standard of living, education, health, work and leisure?
4 Why is the phrase 'your parents and grandparents' repeated so many times in the passage?
5 In which areas have the two older generations admitted failure?

6 What is the actual time gap between (a) you and your parents, and (b) you and your grandparents? How does this time gap stop you from realising what their life was like?

7 Give reasons why you do or do not think that this article is sincere.

8 What has this article done to help you understand the two older generations?

9 Look at the article again with a view to finding out just what kind of person the writer is. Give your opinion in two or three paragraphs.

Summing up

10 State in not more than 50 words the argument in this passage.

Oral ideas

11 *Individual* Give a short talk to the class saying what your attitude is towards any of the following groups of people in authority.

parents   teachers   the police politicians

12 *Individual* Talk to your parents and grandparents about their life when they were your age. Report back to the class what you have discovered.

Writing

13 On behalf of your generation write an effective answer to this passage.

14 Write an essay saying what your generation must do to make the world a better place.

15 Talk to your parents and grandparents about schooling when they were your age. Make notes of what is said. Write a report to be read to the class in session.

16 Write a composition in which you express your appreciation of what the two previous generations have done for you.

17 Write a letter to your local newspaper protesting against something you think is a public nuisance.

Language in use

18 Use a dictionary to find the meaning of each of the following.
epidemic   expectancy   depression
compassion   materialistic   enforce

19 Place each of the following words in well-written sentences.
vitamins   trespassing   ambitions

20 Find synonyms for *paralysis* and *inhabit*.

21 Write out the past tense (3rd person singular) of each of the following:
think   fear   hear   spend
rebuild   find

22 Another way of saying '*double the output per person*' is '*double the per capita output*'. *Per capita* comes from Latin and means '*counting by heads*'. Here are some more words borrowed from Latin. With the help of a good dictionary find the meaning for each one.
agenda   vice versa   bona fide
ad astra   ubique   sub rosa
in absentia   videlicet   in camera
in loco parentis

Activities and research

23 Without the following people your world might have been a very different place. Find out what you can about them from reference books and then write a paragraph about each.
Robert Owen   Richard Henry Tawny
William Beveridge   Richard Austen
Butler   Aneurin Bevan

24 Write an imaginary conversation between either (a) your mother and your grandmother, or (b) your mother and a friend, about yourself and what is to become of you.

25 'When I was your age . . . .' How often have your parents or grandparents said that to you? Try to make a truthful comparison between the life you lead and the life they lived when they were your age.

26 Look at the picture on page 89. Supply a title for it and then describe the scene in not more than 100 words.

SHORT STORY

The short story

People have been telling brief tales for thousands of years. In the beginning they were usually stories about the family and themselves, together with their fights and the magical things that happened to them.

It began long before people could write, so these early stories were not only spoken but also in verse. The rhyme and rhythm of verse made the stories easier to remember and pass on to other people. The *Epic of Gilgamesh*, see page 121, is a good example of such a tale handed down from generation to generation and finally recorded on a clay tablet.

Most of the early stories came from the east. No doubt you have read such tales as *Cain and Abel* (included in the Bible), *The Fables of Aesop*, and *Tales from the Arabian Nights*. The latter is a collection of very ancient oriental tales first put together around 1450 in Cairo, and the first story in this section is a simple version of *The Boy Judge*

taken from that collection.

A good thing about a short story is its shortness. It can be read at one sitting and very often written in the same time. The length of a short story can vary, however, for some people can sit longer than others! What can be said is that this type of fiction may range in length from the 500 words of the short, short story, to the 5,000 words plus of the short story.

In the pages that follow we shall look at a number of short stories. There will be stories to read, followed by questions, and stories to write.

You will be shown how to find ideas for stories, how to plan and organise your material, and how to use language to express your ideas.

And now, *The Boy Judge*, a short story from the very distant past.

The Boy Judge

In the time of the Caliph Haroun, a man called Ali Cogia lived in Baghdad. Ali was not rich: he was a seller of sweets and cakes. But he had no wife and family to look after, and had enough for his own needs.

Under the floor of the room at the back of his shop he kept a jar; and every week he put a small gold piece into it. The money was for him to use when he was old or ill. For, as he often said, 'I have no sons to look after me when I am old and cannot work.'

One day, when Ali was about fifty years old, he took out the jar
10 and counted the money. There were more than a thousand gold pieces inside. 'More than enough for the time when I am old,' he said to himself, and he began to think.

Now, Ali was a good man. He went to the mosque every Friday; he gave money to the poor. But there was one thing which he had not done. He had not made the journey to Mecca.

From that day Ali thought more and more about the journey. He had the money. Poorer men than him had gone. Yet, life in Baghdad was easy, and the road to Mecca was hard. Not everyone who went

20 there came back. But the thought had come into his head and would not go out. The time for the journey was near, and at last he said to his friends: 'This year I will go.'

So he sold his shop and got ready for the journey. But one difficulty remained — the jar with the gold. 'Who will look after it while I am away?' he thought.

At last he thought of something. He went into a shop and bought some olives. Then he filled the jar with them so that they covered the gold. Lastly he closed the top of the jar and took it to his friend Hussein, who kept the shop next to his.

'Brother Hussein,' he said, 'you know that I am going, if God
30 wishes, to Mecca. I have sold everything, and have only this jar of olives. I do not like to waste good food. Can I leave it with you till I come back?'

'That is a small thing to ask a friend,' said Hussein. 'Put it here in this corner of my shop. Nobody will touch it there. And may God bring you safely back to Baghdad.'

After many weeks Ali reached Mecca. There he did all the things that people have to do there. Then the time came for him to leave. This was the first journey that Ali had ever made. Before, he had been afraid to travel. Now, he found that he rather liked it. So he
40 did not go straight back home.

In Mecca he had met some Egyptian merchants. 'Come back with us to Cairo,' they said. 'There is always work there for a maker of sweets.'

So Ali went with them and stayed two years. After that he moved on to Damascus. Time passed. It was nearly seven years since he had left Baghdad.

'It is long enough,' he said one day. 'I shall sell my shop here and go back to my own city of Baghdad to die among my friends.'

On the very day that Ali Cogia left Damascus, Hussein's wife
50 needed some olives. There were none in the house, and the shop in their street was shut. 'What shall I do?' she asked.

'There are some olives in my shop,' said Hussein. 'Do you remember? Seven years ago old Ali Cogia left a jar of them with me. He never came back from Mecca. Some people say he went to Cairo, but he is surely dead by now.'

'So let us eat his olives,' said his wife. 'They are doing no good to a dead man.'

Hussein went into his shop, and there, still in its corner, stood the jar. Nobody had touched it in all those seven years. But when he
60 opened it and looked inside, he saw that the olives at the top were quite dry. He put his hand deeper into the jar, but even those lower down were dry. So he put his whole arm in. When he pulled it out, black, oily and salty, he was holding a gold piece.

He put his hand into the jar again and found more gold. Many thoughts flew round his head. At last he put the gold into the jar again and went back to his wife. To her he only said: 'Those olives were too old and dry.'

The next day he took the olives out of the jar and threw them away. Then he took the gold out and buried it in his yard. Next, he
70 went and bought new olives. He filled the jar with these, and closed it as it had been before.

'Seven years is a long time,' he said to himself, 'but I cannot be sure that Ali Cogia is dead. If he does come back, I shall have a jar of olives to give him. And that is what he asked me to look after — a jar of olives.'

A few weeks later Ali Cogia came back to Baghdad. The first thing he did was to go round to Hussein's house. After they had talked for some time, Ali asked him about the jar of olives.

'Olives?' said Hussein. 'What olives?'

80 'You remember. Before I left, I gave you a jar of olives to keep for me,' said Ali. 'You put it in a corner of your shop.'

'Ah, perhaps you did give me a jar,' said Hussein. 'I had forgotten. Seven years is a long time. Let us go into my shop and see if it is still there.'

Hussein's words had made Ali feel afraid. But when he saw the jar, just where he had left it, he felt much better. 'My friend,' he said, 'you have looked after this jar for seven years. Now I want to give you something. You will see what is in the jar which you have kept so well.'

90 With these words Ali put his arm into the jar and pulled out — not the gold pieces which he wanted to give to Hussein — but olives. He tried again and again, but the same thing happened every time.

'Where is my gold?' he asked at last.

'Gold? What gold?'

'The gold I put in this jar.'

'You said nothing about a jar of gold. You only gave me this jar of olives.'

'My friend, if you needed the money, do not be afraid to say. You may pay it back, a little every week, but . . .'.

100 'I have not touched your jar, and know nothing of any gold . . .'.

At last, after this had gone on for some time, Ali said: 'Enough. I shall go to the judge. He will know which of us is telling the truth, and the law will punish the other.'

'I don't mind,' said Hussein. 'Let us see if the judge is foolish enough to believe the story you have just told me.'

The next day Ali and Hussein took the matter to the judge.

'Did anyone see you put the gold in the jar?' the judge asked Ali.

'No, I was alone. I have no wife or family.'

'Did you tell anybody about putting the gold in the jar?'

110 'No, I did not want anybody to know.'

What did you tell Hussein was in the jar?'

'Olives.'

Then the judge turned to Hussein. 'Did anyone tell you there was gold in this jar?'

'No.'

'Did you at any time open the jar?'

'No.'

'Ali Cogia,' said the judge, 'how can you waste our time in this
way? There is nothing to show that there was ever any gold in your
120   jar. You are an old man. You do not remember what you did seven
years ago.'

Ali was angry at the judge's words. But there was one more thing
he could do. He wrote a letter to the Caliph about the whole matter,
and gave it to one of the Caliph's servants.

By this time the story of the jar of olives had passed through all
the markets of Baghdad. Everybody was talking about it, some
believing Ali, and others believing Hussein. So when the Caliph got
Ali's letter, he read it with care. He liked to know everything that
went on in the city.

130   That night he called for his vizir and said: 'Let us put on plain
clothes tonight and walk about the streets. I want to hear what people
are saying about this Ali Cogia. Is he a fool, or a man of truth, or
a thief?'

As they were walking through that part of the city where Ali lived,
they heard children speak the names of Ali and Hussein.

'You can be Ali.'

'Let me be Hussein.'

'All right, and I shall be the judge.'

The two men stopped and looked into the yard where the voices
140   were coming from. The children were sitting under a tree playing
a game. One boy was playing the judge, and two more were playing
Ali and Hussein. There were others, too. As the game went on, the
Caliph listened more and more carefully. The boy judge was asking
good questions.

At last, the Caliph said to the vizir: 'Go in and speak to this boy.
Tell him to come to the palace tomorrow morning. I also want to see
the judge, Ali Cogia, Hussein, two olive merchants and the jar of
olives.'

The next day all these people came before the Caliph. Every one
150   of them felt afraid: the judge was afraid because he thought he might
have made a mistake; Ali was afraid because the Caliph might think
he *was* a thief; Hussein was afraid because he *was* a thief; the
merchants were afraid because they did not know what the Caliph
might know about them, and the boy was afraid because he had
never seen such a wonderful palace before.

'Come, boy,' said the Caliph. 'Sit down beside me. I heard you
judge these two men in play last night. Today you shall really do it.
— And you,' he said to the judge, 'listen to this child and learn how
to tell truth from untruth, right from wrong, and good men from
160   thieves.'

Although still afraid, the boy spoke clearly. 'Bring me the jar,' he
said. And the jar was put before him. 'Is this the jar you gave to your
friend?'

'Yes,' said Ali.

'Is this the jar that Ali gave to you?'

'Yes,' said Hussein.

The boy put his hand in the jar and took out some olives. He gave some to the Caliph and to Ali and Hussein. Then he slowly ate one himself. 'They are very good olives,' he said.

170 Then to Hussein he said: 'Did you eat any of them before today?'

'Not one,' he answered. 'I did not touch that jar from the time it came into my shop to the day Ali Cogia came back to Baghdad.'

The boy then turned to the olive merchants. 'You try them,' he said. 'They are good olives, although seven years old.'

'Seven years old?' cried one of the merchants. 'I can see by looking at them that they are not so old. They are this year's olives. No olive is any good after three years.'

'Even after two years they lose their colour,' said the second merchant.

180 'And yet Hussein says that these olives have been in the jar for seven years,' said the boy.

'I have bought and sold olives for twenty years,' said the first merchant, 'and I know that olives do not last for seven years.'

Hussein's face had gone white. His eyes were turned to the ground. 'I took the gold,' he said. 'It is in a hole in my yard.'

The Caliph then spoke: 'You know how the law punishes thieves.'

But before Hussein could answer, Ali said: 'O great Caliph, do not cut off his hand. He was once a good friend to me. I did wrong to leave the gold with him. Let him go with a beating.'

190 The Caliph looked at the boy judge. 'A beating would be enough,' the boy said.

'Then let it be so,' said the Caliph.

So Hussein kept his hand, but lost his good name; Ali lost a friend, but got back his gold; and the boy judge was sent by the Caliph to study law. For as the great Haroun said: 'Twenty jars of gold cannot buy a good judge.'

John Turvey
Tales from the Arabian Nights

Understanding

1 What happens in a story is called the plot. Tell in one sentence the plot of *The Boy Judge*.

2 The opening paragraph in a short story should hold the reader's attention and make him want to read on. How far is it true of this story? Give your reasons.

3 Tell, in one paragraph for each, how much we learn about the following characters in the story:
a Alia Cogia
b Hussein
c the boy judge

4 Where a story takes place is called the setting. Write a paragraph about the setting for *The Boy Judge*.

5 How did the jar of olives cause a problem for Hussein? How did the problem arise and what was his answer to it?

6 What problem faced Ali Cogia on his return from his travels? Explain what happened and how Ali Cogia tried to solve the problem.

7 Why is the boy judge introduced into the story?

8 Many of these ancient tales from the east end with a moral: that is a lesson that can be learned by the reader from the story. Tell in your own words what you think is the moral of this story.

Writing

9 Write a different ending for *The Boy Judge*. Start with the Caliph and his vizir out for their evening walk and hearing the children playing their game. The Caliph makes a mistake and chooses the wrong boy: the one who plays Hussein. Tell what happens in court.

10 The Bible contains many short, short stories. These stories were used to teach the listener or reader in an interesting way. Here is one of them, the story of *The Good Samaritan* from the New Testament. Read it carefully and then do the exercise.

A man was travelling from Jerusalem to Jericho, along a lonely road, when he was attacked by a gang of robbers who beat him almost to death and escaped with all his money.

A priest happened to be travelling along the same road, and when he saw the man's beaten body lying by the roadside, he crossed to the other side of the road and passed by without stopping. Some time afterwards one of the Temple assistants also came along the road, and seeing the injured man he too crossed over and passed on the other side.

Then a third man came along, a Samaritan. When he saw the man lying there, he felt very sorry for him. Kneeling down he washed his wounds with the wine and oil he was carrying and bandaged them. Then he lifted the man on to his own horse and took him to the nearest inn. He gave the innkeeper some money and instructed him. 'Look after this man. On my return

journey I will call in and if you have had any additional expense I will make it good.'

from *A Child's Bible: New Testament*
rewritten by Shirley Steen

Tell this story as if it took place today. Remember that:

a the two people who pass by the injured person are supposed to be 'good',

b the 'Samaritan' who stopped to help was a member of a group looked down upon by the Jews,

c your story must start with the first sentence and go straight through to the end in as few words as possible,

d your version should be a 200 word, very short story of the same length as the original.

Start with the following if you cannot think of an opening:

A girl/boy was travelling home from a disco, along a lonely road, when he/she was attacked by muggers . . .

11 It is important that the beginning of a short story be right. That first sentence and first paragraph must take the reader straight into the story, make an impact and create the right mood or atmosphere. Here are some openings to short stories. Improve them if you can and then write the first paragraph they introduce.

The door closed, leaving her in a strange darkness.

Her body rocked with crying but there was no sound.

He stopped writing and closed the book.

12 Write a short story suggested to you by the picture on this page.

The critics

13 Let your teacher choose the best three opening paragraphs written for question 12. Say what is successful or unsuccessful about each paragraph and comment on any assessment made by your teacher.

The Gift

Tomorrow would be Christmas and even while the three of them rode to the rocket port, the mother and father were worried. It was the boy's first flight into space, his very first time in a rocket, and they wanted everything to be perfect. So when, at the customs table, they were forced to leave behind his gift which exceeded the weight limit by no more than a few ounces and the little tree with the lovely white candles, they felt themselves deprived of the season and their love.

The boy was waiting for them in the Terminal room. Walking
10 towards him, after their unsuccessful clash with the Interplanetary officials, the mother and father whispered to each other.

'What shall we do?'

'Nothing, nothing. What *can* we do?'

'Silly rules!'

'And he so wanted the tree!'

The siren gave a great howl and people pressed forward into the Mars Rocket. The mother and father walked at the very last, their small pale son between them, silent.

'I'll think of something,' said the father.

20 'What . . .?' asked the boy.

And the rocket took off and they were flung headlong into dark space.

The rocket moved and left fire behind and left Earth behind on which the date was December 24th, 2052, heading out into a place where there was no time at all, no month, no year, no hour. They slept away the rest of the first 'day'. Near midnight, by their Earth-time New York watches, the boy awoke and said, 'I want to go look out the porthole.'

There was only one port, a 'window' of immensely thick glass, of
30 some size, up on the next deck.

'Not quite yet,' said the father. 'I'll take you up later.'

'I want to see where we are and where we're going.'

'I want you to wait, for a reason,' said the father.

He had been lying awake, turning this way and that, thinking of the abandoned gift, the problem of the season, the lost tree and the white candles. And at last, sitting up, no more than five minutes ago, he believed he had found a plan. He need only carry it out and this journey would be fine and joyous indeed.

'Son,' he said, 'in exactly one half-hour it will be Christmas.'

40 'Oh,' said the mother, dismayed that he had mentioned it. Somehow she had rather hoped the boy would forget.

The boy's face grew feverish and his lips trembled. 'I know, I know. Will I get a present, will I? Will I have a tree ? You promised ——'

'Yes, yes, all that, and more,' said the father.

The mother started. 'But ——'

'I mean it,' said the father. 'I really mean it. All and more, much

more. Excuse me, now. I'll be back.'

He left them for about twenty minutes. When he came back he
50   was smiling. 'Almost time.'

'Can I hold your watch?' asked the boy, and the watch was handed
over and he held it ticking in his fingers as the rest of the hour drifted
by in fire and silence and unfelt motion.

'It's Christmas *now*! Christmas! Where's my present?'

'Here we go,' said the father, and took his boy by the shoulder and
led him from the room, down the hall, up a rampway, his wife
following.

'I don't understand,' she kept saying.

'You will. Here we are,' said the father.

60   They had stopped at the closed door of a large cabin. The father
tapped three times and then twice, in a code. The door opened and
the light in the cabin went out and there was a whisper of voices.

'Go on in, son,' said the father.

'It's dark.'

'I'll hold your hand. Come on, mama.'

They stepped into the room and the door shut, and the room was
very dark indeed. And before them loomed a great glass eye, the
porthole, a window four feet high and six feet wide, from which they
could look out into space.

70   The boy gasped.

Behind him, the father and the mother gasped with him, and then
in the dark room some people began to sing.

'Merry Christmas, son,' said the father.

And the voices in the room sang the old, the familiar carols, and
the boy moved forward slowly until his face was pressed against the
cool glass of the port. And he stood there for a long long time, just
looking and looking out into space and the deep night at the burning
and the burning of ten billion billion white and lovely candles . . .

Ray Bradbury

Understanding

1 Tell in one sentence the plot of this story.

2 What is the setting for *The Gift*? Is this setting effective? Give reasons for your answer.

3 Look at the sentence 'The rocket moved . . . no hour', lines 23–25. Tell in your own words what you think the writer has tried to do here.

4 Look at the dialogue (speech) between mother and father in lines 12–15 and then answer these questions:

a What kind of a mood are both parents in?

b Why is *can* printed in italic?

c Which lines are spoken by the mother and which by the father?

5 What do we learn about the characters of the mother, the father and the son, from their speech?

6 Who tells the story of *The Gift*? Is it (a) one of the characters in the story, or (b) someone who doesn't appear in the story but knows everything about everyone?

7 Choose from this list the kind of ending Ray Bradbury has used for *The Gift*. One that:

a solves a problem

b answers a mystery

c shows change in a character

d makes a situation clear

e has a twist in the tale

Say whether or not you think Bradbury's ending is a good one.

Writing

8 We have seen in question 4 that speech in a story is called dialogue and can be used to show the moods of characters. Write six lines of dialogue between any two people of your own choice showing the moods that both of them are in.

9 It is quite possible that you will be alive to celebrate Christmas in 2052. Write the dialogue that might take place between yourself and a child in the house, about Christmas when you were young.

10 Look at question 6. If the answer is 'a' then the story was told in the *first person*. If the answer is 'b' then the story was told in the *third person*. Check with your teacher to make sure of this.

11 It is better to tell your stories in the third person for then you show your readers by action. If you use the first person you may be tempted to tell your readers about your characters and this makes for dull writing. Remember, it is better to *show* readers that a character is angry than to *tell* them. Write a short, short story about a quarrel scene between two characters and *show* by the dialogue that each is angry.

12 Always ask yourself if the story you are going to write can be told with just two or three characters. Few characters are needed to tell a short story.

Write a story about an aircraft crash on a desert island and what happened to *not more* than three survivors.

13 Write a short, short story about *one* character. Tell of that character's appearance, show that character in action, and reveal that character in speech. Show the personality of this figure. It could well be a friend, a created character, or even yourself.

14 Write a short story in the third person telling of the life of Bradbury's father, mother and son on Mars after a number of years. It is often a good idea to start a story with a conversation and you may use the following or one of your own.

'Was earth really green and watery?'

Boy looked to his mother.

'Were there green mornings when the earth was freshly washed after rain?'

Boy had been on Mars now for six years and memories of Earth were fading.

The Umbrella Man

I'm going to tell you about a funny thing that happened to my
mother and me yesterday evening. I am twelve years old and I'm a
girl. My mother is thirty-four but I am nearly as tall as her already.

Yesterday afternoon, my mother took me up to London to see the
dentist. He found one hole. It was in a back tooth and he filled it
without hurting me too much. After that, we went to a café. I had
a banana split and my mother had a cup of coffee. By the time we
got up to leave, it was about six o'clock.

When we came out of the café it had started to rain. 'We must get
10 a taxi,' my mother said. We were wearing ordinary hats and coats,
and it was raining quite hard.

'Why don't we go back into the café and wait for it to stop?' I said.
I wanted another of those banana splits. They were gorgeous.

'It isn't going to stop,' my mother said. 'We must get home.'

We stood on the pavement in the rain, looking for a taxi. Lots of
them came by but they all had passengers inside them. 'I wish we
had a car with a chauffeur,' my mother said.

Just then, a man came up to us. He was a small man and he was
pretty old, probably seventy or more. He raised his hat politely and
20 said to my mother, 'Excuse me. I do hope you will excuse me
. . .' He had a fine white moustache and bushy white eyebrows
and a wrinkly pink face. He was sheltering under an umbrella
which he held high over his head.

'Yes?' my mother said, very cool and distant.

'I wonder if I could ask a small favour of you,' he said. 'It is only
a very small favour.'

I saw my mother looking at him suspiciously. She is a suspicious
person, my mother. She is especially suspicious of two things —
strange men and boiled eggs. When she cuts the top off a boiled egg,
30 she pokes around inside it with her spoon as though expecting to find
a mouse or something. With strange men, she has a golden rule
which says, 'The nicer the man seems to be, the more suspicious you
must become.' This little old man was particularly nice. He was
polite. He was well-spoken. He was well-dressed. He was a real
gentleman. The reason I knew he was a gentleman was because of
his shoes. 'You can always spot a gentleman by the shoes he wears,'
was another of my mother's favourite sayings. This man had
beautiful brown shoes.

'The truth of the matter is,' the little man was saying, 'I've got
40 myself into a bit of a scrape. I need some help. Not much, I assure
you. It's almost nothing, in fact, but I do need it. You see, madam,
old people like me often become terribly forgetful . . .'

My mother's chin was up and she was staring down at him along
the full length of her nose. It is a fearsome thing, this frosty-nosed
stare of my mother's. Most people go to pieces completely when she
gives it to them. I once saw my own headmistress begin to stammer
and simper like an idiot when my mother gave her a really foul

frosty-noser. But the little man on the pavement with the umbrella over his head didn't bat an eyelid. He gave a gentle smile and said, 'I beg you to believe, madam, that I am not in the habit of stopping ladies in the street and telling them my troubles.'

'I should hope not,' my mother said.

I felt quite embarrassed by my mother's sharpness. I wanted to say to her, 'Oh, mummy, for heaven's sake, he's a very very old man, and he's sweet and polite, and he's in some sort of trouble, so don't be so beastly to him.' But I didn't say anything.

The little man shifted his umbrella from one hand to the other. 'I've never forgotten it before,' he said.

'You've never forgotten what?' my mother asked sternly.

'My wallet,' he said. 'I must have left it in my other jacket. Isn't that the silliest thing to do?'

'Are you asking me to give you money?' my mother said.

'Oh, good gracious me, no!' he cried. 'Heaven forbid I should ever do that!'

'Then what *are* you asking?' my mother said. 'Do hurry up. We're getting soaked to the skin standing here.'

'I know you are,' he said. 'And that is why I'm offering you this umbrella of mine to protect you and to keep forever if . . . if only . . .'

'If only what?' my mother said.

'If only you would give me in return a pound for my taxi-fare just to get me home.'

My mother was still suspicious. 'If you had no money in the first place,' she said, 'then how did you get here?'

'I walked,' he answered. 'Every day I go for a lovely long walk and then I summon a taxi to take me home. I do it every day of the year.'

'Why don't you walk home now?' my mother asked.

'Oh, I wish I could,' he said. 'I do wish I could. But I don't think I could manage it on these silly old legs of mine. I've gone too far already.'

My mother stood there chewing her lower lip. She was beginning to melt a bit, I could see that. And the idea of getting an umbrella to shelter under must have tempted her a good deal.

'It's a lovely umbrella,' the little man said.

'So I've noticed,' my mother said.

'It's silk,' he said.

'I can see that.'

'Then why don't you take it, madam,' he said. 'It cost me over twenty pounds. I promise you. But that's of no importance so long as I can get home and rest these old legs of mine.'

I saw my mother's hand feeling for the clasp on her purse. She saw me watching her. I was giving her one of my *own* frosty-nosed looks this time and she knew exactly what I was telling her. Now listen, mummy, I was telling her, you simply *mustn't* take advantage of a tired old man in this way. It's a rotten thing to do. My mother paused and looked back at me. Then she said to the little man, 'I don't think it's quite right that I should take a silk umbrella from you worth twenty pounds. I think I'd just better *give* you the taxi-fare and be done with it.'

100 'No, no, no!' he cried. 'It's out of the question! I wouldn't dream of it! Not in a million years! I would never accept money from you like that! Take the umbrella, dear lady, and keep the rain off your shoulders!'

My mother gave me a triumphant sideways look. There you are, she was telling me. You're wrong. He *wants* me to have it.

She fished into her purse and took out a pound note. She held it out to the little man. He took it and handed her the umbrella. He pocketed the pound, raised his hat, gave a quick bow from the waist, and said, 'Thank you, madam, thank you.' Then he was gone.

110 'Come under here and keep dry, darling,' my mother said. 'Aren't we lucky, I've never had a silk umbrella before. I couldn't afford it.'

'Why were you so horrid to him in the beginning?' I asked.

'I wanted to satisfy myself he wasn't a trickster,' she said. 'And I did. He was a gentleman. I'm very pleased I was able to help him.'

'Yes, mummy,' I said.

'A *real* gentleman,' she went on. 'Wealthy, too, otherwise he wouldn't have had a silk umbrella. I shouldn't be surprised if he isn't a titled person. Sir Harry Goldsworthy or something like that.'

'Yes, mummy.'

120 'This will be a good lesson to you,' she went on. 'Never rush things. Always take your time when you are summing someone up. Then you'll never make mistakes.'

'There he goes,' I said. 'Look.'

'Where?'

'Over there. He's crossing the street. Goodness, mummy, what a hurry he's in.'

We watched the little man as he dodged nimbly in and out of the traffic. When he reached the other side of the street, he turned left, walking very fast.

130 'He doesn't look very tired to me, does he to you, mummy?'

My mother didn't answer.

'He doesn't look as though he's trying to get a taxi, either.' I said.

My mother was standing very still and stiff, staring across the street at the little man. We could see him clearly. He was in a terrific hurry. He was bustling along the pavement, sidestepping the other pedestrians and swinging his arms like a soldier on the march.

'He's up to something,' my mother said, stony-faced.

'But what?'

'I don't know,' my mother snapped. 'But I'm going to find out.

140 Come with me.' She took my arm and we crossed the street together. Then we turned left.

'Can you see him?' my mother asked.

'Yes. There he is. He's turning right down the next street.'

We came to the corner and turned right. The little man was about twenty yards ahead of us. He was scuttling along like a rabbit and

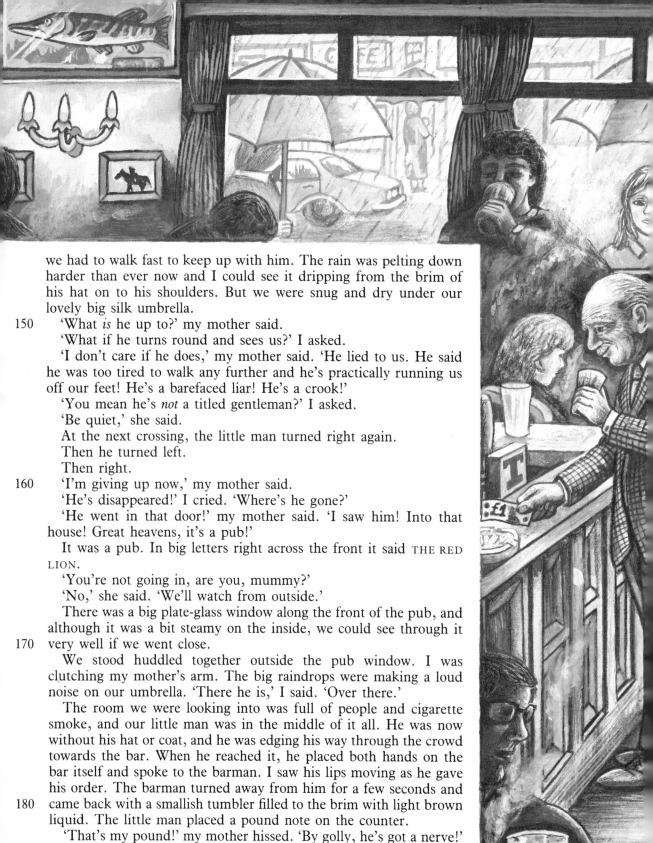

we had to walk fast to keep up with him. The rain was pelting down harder than ever now and I could see it dripping from the brim of his hat on to his shoulders. But we were snug and dry under our lovely big silk umbrella.

150   'What *is* he up to?' my mother said.

'What if he turns round and sees us?' I asked.

'I don't care if he does,' my mother said. 'He lied to us. He said he was too tired to walk any further and he's practically running us off our feet! He's a barefaced liar! He's a crook!'

'You mean he's *not* a titled gentleman?' I asked.

'Be quiet,' she said.

At the next crossing, the little man turned right again.

Then he turned left.

Then right.

160   'I'm giving up now,' my mother said.

'He's disappeared!' I cried. 'Where's he gone?'

'He went in that door!' my mother said. 'I saw him! Into that house! Great heavens, it's a pub!'

It was a pub. In big letters right across the front it said THE RED LION.

'You're not going in, are you, mummy?'

'No,' she said. 'We'll watch from outside.'

There was a big plate-glass window along the front of the pub, and although it was a bit steamy on the inside, we could see through it 170 very well if we went close.

We stood huddled together outside the pub window. I was clutching my mother's arm. The big raindrops were making a loud noise on our umbrella. 'There he is,' I said. 'Over there.'

The room we were looking into was full of people and cigarette smoke, and our little man was in the middle of it all. He was now without his hat or coat, and he was edging his way through the crowd towards the bar. When he reached it, he placed both hands on the bar itself and spoke to the barman. I saw his lips moving as he gave his order. The barman turned away from him for a few seconds and 180 came back with a smallish tumbler filled to the brim with light brown liquid. The little man placed a pound note on the counter.

'That's my pound!' my mother hissed. 'By golly, he's got a nerve!'

'What's in the glass?' I asked.

'Whisky,' my mother said. 'Neat whisky.'

The barman didn't give him any change from the pound.

'That must be a treble whisky,' my mother said.

'What's a treble?' I asked.

'Three times the normal measure,' she answered.

190 The little man picked up the glass and put it to his lips. He tilted it gently. Then he tilted it higher . . . and higher . . . and higher . . . and very soon all the whisky had disappeared down his throat in one long pour.

'That was a jolly expensive drink,' I said.

'It's ridiculous!' my mother said. 'Fancy paying a pound for something you swallow in one go!'

'It cost him more than a pound,' I said. 'It cost him a twenty-pound silk umbrella.'

'So it did,' my mother said. 'He must be mad.'

The little man was standing by the bar with the empty glass in his
200 hand. He was smiling now, and a sort of golden glow of pleasure was spreading over his round pink face. I saw his tongue come out to lick the white moustache, as though searching for the last drop of that precious whisky.

Slowly, he turned away from the bar and edged back through the crowd to where his hat and coat were hanging. He put on his hat. He put on his coat. Then, in a manner so superbly cool and casual that you hardly noticed anything at all, he lifted from the coat-rack one of the many wet umbrellas hanging there, and off he went.

'Did you see that!' my mother shrieked. 'Did you see what he did!'
210 'Ssshh!' I whispered. 'He's coming out!'

We lowered the umbrella to hide our faces, and peeped out from under it.

Out he came. But he never looked in our direction. He opened his new umbrella over his head and scurried off down the road the way he had come.

'So that's his little game!' my mother said.

'Neat,' I said. 'Super.'

We followed him back to the main street where we had first met him, and we watched him as he proceeded, with no trouble at all,
220 to exchange his new umbrella for another pound note. This time it was with a tall thin fellow who didn't even have a coat or hat. And as soon as the transaction was completed, our little man trotted off down the street and was lost in the crowd. But this time he went in the opposite direction.

'You see how clever he is!' my mother said. 'He never goes to the same pub twice!'

'He could go on doing this all night,' I said.

'Yes,' my mother said. 'Of course. But I'll bet he plays like mad for rainy days.'

Roald Dahl

107

Understanding

1 *The Umbrella Man* is a traditional short story with this classic shape. Note that there is a slow build-up to the climax and then a rapid falling off.

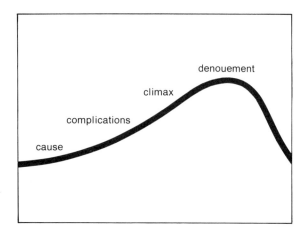

Cause, complications, climax and *denouement* (explanation or outcome) in *The Umbrella Man* are as follows:

cause of situation

mother and daughter in London for daughter's dental appointment

complications

a it rains and there is no taxi
b little man, too tired to walk, offers umbrella for £1
c man takes money and hurries away in a suspicious manner

climax

man enters pub and buys large whisky with money

denouement

man steals umbrella in pub to obtain another pound and more whisky

2 Read once again *The Boy Judge* and *The Gift*. For each story give the *cause, complications, climax* and *denouement* as in the example above for *The Umbrella Man*.

Writing

3 In *The Umbrella Man* both mother and daughter thought the little old man 'a real gentleman' because he was polite, well-spoken and well-dressed. In not more than 200 words write a description of someone who was *not* 'a real gentleman'.

4 Try to remember some problem in your life, or in that of a friend, and turn it into a short story. Write in the third person and use the same shape as that for *The Umbrella Man*.

5 Write a short story for a younger brother or sister.

6 Here are six headlines from newspapers. Use *one* of them as a title and then write the short story to go with it.

> Student Digs Out of Cave After Six Days
> Panic in Los Angeles
> Who Cares Now if it Snows?
> Nurse Saves 86 Patients
> Bulbs Instead of Onions in Soup
> Entire Town Joins Search

7 Find three items in the news which you think could be used as short stories. Paste each on a separate sheet of paper and beneath the item outline the plot in a sentence and go on to give the cause, complications, climax and denouement of the short story you could write.

8 Here are some different types of short story. Choose one in which you are interested and try your hand at writing that kind of story.

> adventure   mystery   animal
> humorous   love   science-fiction

9 Here in one sentence is the plot of Shakespeare's *Macbeth*:

A general, in order to become king, murders the king and seizes the throne, but is finally killed by the murdered king's sons and their friends.

Use this plot, set in any part of the world, for a short story of your own.

His First Flight

The young sea-gull was alone on his ledge. His two brothers and his sister had already flown away the day before. He had been afraid to fly with them. Somehow, when he had taken a little run forward to the brink of the ledge and attempted to flap his wings, he became afraid. The great expanse of sea stretched down beneath, and it was such a long way down — miles down. He felt certain that his wings would never support him, so he bent his head and ran away to the little hole under the ledge where he slept at night.

Even when each of his brothers and his little sister, whose wings were far shorter than his own, ran to the brink, flapped their wings, and flew away, he failed to muster up courage to take that plunge which appeared to him so desperate. His father and mother had come around calling to him shrilly, upbraiding him, threatening to let him starve on his ledge unless he flew away. But for the life of him he could not move.

That was twenty-four hours ago. Since then nobody had come near him. The day before, all day long he had watched his parents flying about with his brothers and sister, perfecting them in the art of flight, teaching them how to skim the waves and how to dive for fish. He had, in fact, seen his older brother catch his first herring and devour it, standing on a rock, while his parents circled around raising a proud cackle. And all the morning the whole family had walked about on the big plateau mid-way down the opposite cliff, taunting him with his cowardice.

The sun was now ascending the sky, blazing warmly on his ledge that faced the south. He felt the heat because he had not eaten since the previous nightfall. Then he had found a dried piece of mackerel's tail at the far end of his ledge. Now there was not a single scrap of food left. He had searched every inch, rooting among the rough, dirt-caked straw nest where he and his brothers and sister had been hatched. He even gnawed at the dried pieces of spotted egg-shell. It was like eating part of himself.

He had then trotted back and forth from one end of the ledge to the other, his grey body the colour of the cliff, his long grey legs stepping daintily, trying to find some means of reaching his parents without having to fly. But on each side of him the ledge ended in a sheer fall of precipice, with the sea beneath. And between him and his parents there was a deep, wide chasm.

Surely he could reach them without flying, if he could only move northwards along the cliff-face? But then, on what could he walk? There was no ledge, and he was not a fly. And above him he could see nothing. The precipice was sheer, and the top of it was perhaps further away than the sea beneath him.

He stepped slowly out to the brink of the ledge, and, standing on one leg with the other leg hidden under his wing, he closed one eye, then the other, and pretended he was falling asleep. Still they took no notice of him. He saw his brothers and his sister lying on the

plateau dozing, with their heads sunk into their necks. His father was preening the feathers on his white back. Only his mother was looking
50 at him.

She was standing on a little high hump on the plateau, her white breast thrust forward. Now and again she tore at a piece of fish that lay at her feet, and then scraped each side of her beak on the rock. The sight of the food maddened him. How he loved to tear food that way, scraping his beak now and again to whet it! He uttered a low cackle. His mother cackled too, and looked over at him.

'Ga, ga, ga,' he cried, begging her to bring him over some food. 'Gawl-ool-ah,' she screamed back derisively. But he kept calling plaintively, and after a minute or so he uttered a joyful scream. His
60 mother had picked up a piece of the fish and was flying across to him with it. He leaned out eagerly, tapping the rock with his feet, trying to get nearer to her as she flew across. But when she was just opposite to him, abreast of the ledge, she halted, her legs hanging limp, her wings motionless, the piece of fish in her beak almost within reach of his beak.

He waited a moment in surprise, wondering why she did not come nearer, and then, maddened by hunger, he dived at the fish. With a loud scream he fell outwards and downwards into space. His mother had swooped upwards. As he passed beneath her he heard
70 the swish of her wings.

Then a monstrous terror seized him and his heart stood still. He could hear nothing. But it only lasted a moment. The next moment he felt his wings spread outwards. The wind rushed against his breast feathers, then under his stomach and against his wings. He could feel the tips of his wings cutting through the air. He was not falling headlong now. He was soaring gradually downwards and outwards. He was no longer afraid. He just felt a bit dizzy. Then he flapped his wings once and he soared upwards.

He uttered a joyous scream and flapped them again. He soared
80 higher. He raised his breast and banked against the wind. 'Ga, ga, ga. Ga, ga, ga. Gawl-ool-ah.' His mother swooped past him, her wings making a loud noise. He answered her with another scream. Then his father flew over him screaming. Then he saw his two brothers and sister flying around him, curvetting and banking and soaring and diving.

Then he completely forgot that he had not always been able to fly, and commenced himself to dive and soar and curvet, shrieking shrilly.

He was near the sea now, flying straight over it, facing out over
90 the ocean. He saw a vast green sea beneath him, with little ridges moving over it, and he turned his beak sideways and crowed amusedly. His parents and his brothers and sister had landed on this green floor in front of him. They were beckoning to him, calling shrilly. He dropped his legs to stand on the green sea. His legs sank into it. He screamed with fright and attempted to rise again, flapping his wings. But he was tired and weak with hunger and he could not

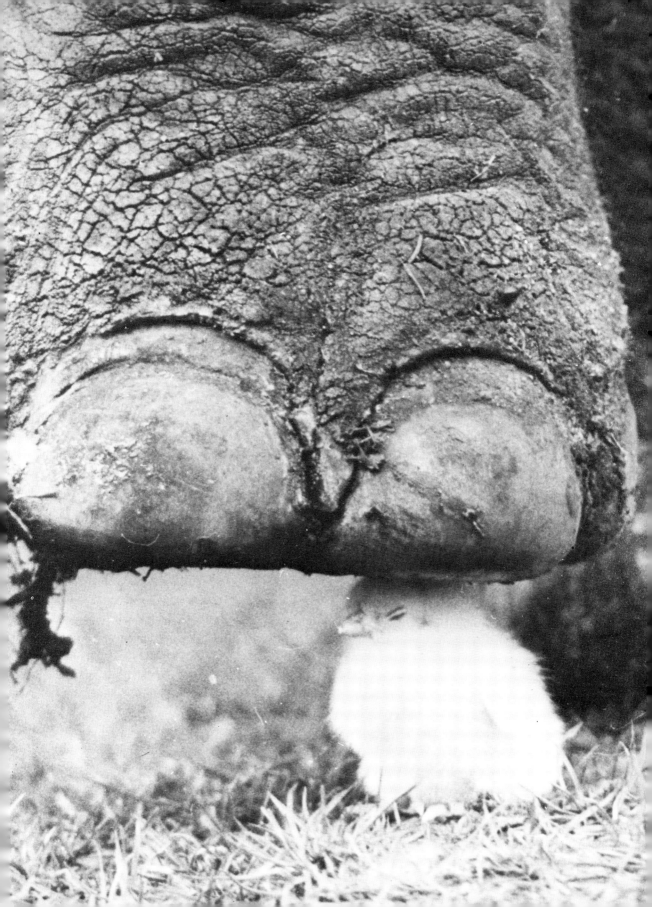

rise, exhausted by the strange exercise. His feet sank into the green sea, and then his belly touched it and he sank no farther.

100   He was floating on it. And around him his family was screaming, praising him, and their beaks were offering him scraps of dog-fish. He had made his first flight.

Liam O'Flaherty

Understanding

1 Tell in one sentence the plot of this story.

2 The young sea-gull has been given human qualities. For example, he is accused of the human quality of cowardice and evidence of this is given. Find in the story other human qualities given to the young sea-gull and the evidence to support them.

3 In your own words, describe in as much detail as you can, the setting in which this story takes place.

4 Tell the story of *His First Flight* through the eyes of the young sea-gull's mother.

5 How did the young bird's brothers, sister and father react to him because of his fear?

6 How did the young sea-gull react to the way his family treated him?

7 What did the sea-gulls look like? How good is the description of them? Give examples to prove what you are saying.

8 In one sentence say what you think of the 'conversation' between the young sea-gull and his mother.

9 How good are the descriptions of the flights of the birds? Give examples and your reasons for choosing them.

Writing

10 Write a story about something you had to do for the first time, e.g. learning to swim, and say how you managed to overcome that problem and your fear.

11 Write an animal or bird story similar to *His First Flight*. Give the animal or bird human qualities and a problem that has to be met and solved.

12 Write a short story suggested to you by the animal picture on page 111.

13 Study the picture opposite. Place one or two characters in this kind of setting and develop it into a short story.

14 One way to plan a short story is to sort your ideas into three parts:

Part one   Outline your chief character, his position in life and his problem. When your reader has finished this part of the story he should be wondering how on earth your character is going to sort out his life.

Part two   Increase the suspense of your reader by bringing in new problems so that your character's task now seems impossible to solve.

Part three   Bring the story to a climax where your chief character's problems will all be solved. Make sure there is a reasonable and believable ending to the story, even if you choose a surprise climax.

Use this kind of plan to make notes on a short story of your own choosing.

The critics

15 Choose any one of the stories in this section and say what you thought about it. Discuss its good points and its faults. Quote from the story to support your view.

16 Ask your teacher to choose the three best short stories written in answer to question 13. Have them read aloud and then discuss what is successful and what is unsuccessful about each one. You might also decide whether or not your teacher's comment is on the right lines!

17 Discuss the choice of stories in this section.

PLAYSCRIPT

Noah

by André Obey

Introduction

When the Lord saw how wicked everyone on earth was and how evil their thoughts were all the time, he was sorry that he had ever made them and put them on earth.

He was so filled with regret that he said, 'I will wipe out these people I have created, and also the animals and the birds, because I am sorry that I made any of them.'

But the Lord was pleased with Noah.

God said to Noah, 'I have decided to put an end to all mankind. I will destroy them completely, because the world is full of their violent deeds. Build a boat for yourself out of good timber . . .'

Genesis 6

115

So Noah began to build his boat of good timber on dry desert land, miles from any river and hundreds of miles from any sea. Hammering, sawing and pounding, he built a boat 450 feet long (133 metres), 75 feet wide (22 metres), and 3 storeys high (13 metres). At the top there was a small window, whilst at the side there was a door big enough for two elephants side by side and tall enough for two giraffes.

The Ark towered dark and huge over Noah's village. At first his neighbours thought it funny, but later they became worried. Strangers came from miles around to laugh at this crazy man who was building the world's biggest boat in the middle of the desert. To his neighbours Noah was a fool, but also a dangerous fool. Even his sons and their girl friends were treated as figures of fun, for they were to become the crew of a dry-land boat.

Does the Ark need a rudder?

But Noah had other things to worry about. God had ordered him to build the Ark, but had not given detailed plans. There were times when Noah needed advice. Here he is talking to God, asking whether or not the Ark ought to have a rudder. It is the opening scene of the play *Noah* by André Obey.

Extract 1

A glade. The Ark is at the right, only the poop deck showing, with a ladder to the ground. NOAH *is taking measurements and singing a little song. He scratches his head and goes over the measurements again. Then he calls:*

NOAH (*softly*) Lord . . . (*Louder*) Lord . . . (*Very loud*) Lord! . . . Yes, Lord, it's me. Extremely sorry to bother You again, but . . . What's that? Yes, I know You've other things to think of, but after I've once shoved off, won't it be a little late? . . . Oh, no, Lord, no, no, no . . . No, Lord, please don't think that. . . . Oh, but naturally, of course, I trust You! You could tell me to set sail on a plank — a branch — on just a cabbage leaf. . . . Yes, You could even tell me to put out to sea with nothing but my loincloth, even without my loincloth — completely — (*He has gone down on his knees, but he gets up immediately*) Yes, yes, Lord, I beg Your pardon. I know Your time is precious. Well, this is all I wanted to ask You: Should I make a rudder? I say, a rudder. . . . No, no, Lord. R for Robert; U for Una; D for . . . that's it, a rudder. Good . . . very good, I never thought of that. Of course, winds, currents, tides . . . What was that, Lord? Storms? Oh, and while You're there just one other little thing. . . . Are You listening, Lord? (*To the audience*) Gone!! . . . He's in a bad temper. . . . Well, you can't blame Him; He has so much to think of. All right; no rudder. (*He considers the Ark*) Tides, currents, winds. (*He imitates the winds*) Psch! . . . Psch! . . .

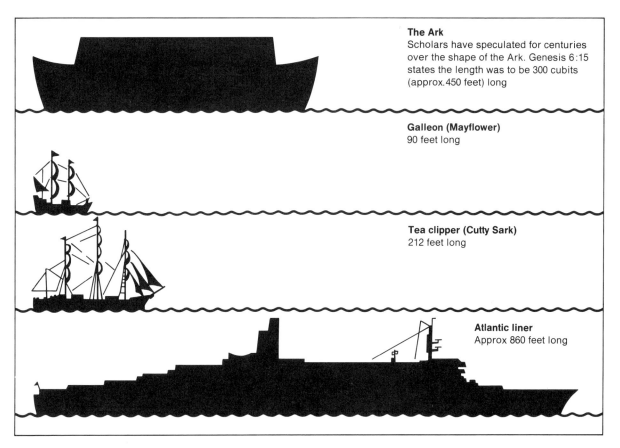

The Ark
Scholars have speculated for centuries over the shape of the Ark. Genesis 6:15 states the length was to be 300 cubits (approx.450 feet) long

Galleon (Mayflower)
90 feet long

Tea clipper (Cutty Sark)
212 feet long

Atlantic liner
Approx 860 feet long

▲ *Shape and size of the Ark*

Storms. (*He imitates the tempests*) Vloum! Be da Bloum! Oh, that's going to be (*he makes a quick movement*) simply . . . magnificent!! . . . No, no, Lord, I'm not afraid. I know that You'll be with me. I was only trying to imagine. . . . Oh, Lord, while You're there I'd like just to ask . . . (*To the audience*) Che! Gone again. You see how careful you have to be. (*He laughs*) He was listening all the time. (*He goes to the Ark*) Storms! . . . I think I'll just put a few more nails in down here. (*He hammers and sings*)

When the boat goes well, all goes well.
When all goes well, the boat goes well.

(*He admires his work*) And when I think that a year ago I couldn't hammer a nail without hitting my thumb. That's pretty good, if I do say so myself. (*He climbs aboard the Ark and stands there like a captain*) Larboard and starboard! . . . Cast off the hawsers! . . . Close the portholes! . . . 'Ware shoals! . . . Wait till the squall's over! . . . Now I'm ready, completely ready, absolutely ready! I'm ready. (*He cries to Heaven*) I am ready! (*Then quietly*) Well, I should like to know how all this business is going to begin. (*He looks all around, at the trees, the bushes, and the sky*) Magnificent weather — oppressively hot and no sign of a cloud. Well, that part of the programme is His look-out.

117

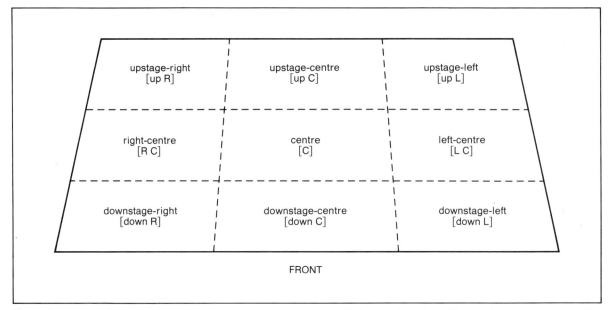

upstage-right [up R]	upstage-centre [up C]	upstage-left [up L]
right-centre [R C]	centre [C]	left-centre [L C]
downstage-right [down R]	downstage-centre [down C]	downstage-left [down L]

FRONT

Looking at the scene

1 How does Noah speak to God? Choose *three* words from this list to describe his way of speaking:

angrily   simply   happily   hastily
timidly   conversationally

Look at the speech again and say why you have chosen these three words.

2 What *kind* of speech does Noah make to God? Is it:

bitter   anxious   boring   amusing
exciting   childlike

Choose *three* of these words and then look at the speech to say why you have chosen them.

3 What kind of person is Noah? Choose *two* of the following words that describe him:

foolish   serious   educated   simple
trusting   lazy   easy-going   comic

4 Tell in *two* separate paragraphs of your own words what you have learnt from this scene about (a) Noah, and (b) God.

Setting

5 The stage of most theatres is divided into the nine areas shown in the plan above.

Make a drawing like this, *leaving out the names of the areas*, to show how a stage would look when Noah is talking to God. Remember that there is a glade or open space, that there are trees and shrubs, and that the Ark is on the right with just the top half showing.

Will you place the Ark at upstage-right or at right-centre? And where on stage will be the glade and shrubs?

Playreading

6 Form groups of four in order to look at Noah's speech to God. Take turns to read the speech. Choose the best in each group to give the speech to the class for comment.

The legend of the flood

7 Read carefully the story of Noah's flood in any Bible. It can be found in Genesis 6, 7 and 8. Note that Obey has changed the story and made Ham, Shem and Japheth much younger and with girl friends instead of wives. Can you think of reasons why he should have done this?

The animals and neighbours arrive

Soon the neighbours of Noah had more to worry about. Wild and fierce beasts — lions, leopards, crocodiles and slimy, slithering, crawly things — began to wander through the fields and up the ramp that led to the big door of the Ark. Mixed with them were such tame animals as cows, pigs and sheep, whilst from overhead came the sound of wings as birds of all kinds and sizes flew towards the boat.

The villagers were alarmed. Noah must be evil, for no one could control animals like that unless he practised black magic. The whole thing had to be stopped: it had gone far enough. A crowd, shouting and waving their arms, gathered outside Noah's house, whilst others made their way towards the Ark.

Meanwhile, with all the animals on board, the family of Noah arrived to complete the crew: his wife; his sons Shem, Ham and Japheth; and their girl friends Ada, Sella and Naomi.

The first neighbour to reach the Ark was a man. He accused Noah of stealing the animals and of causing the terrible drought, and then threatened the old man with a spear. Noah called upon God to prove that he was right and then the rain began to fall.

Extract 2

NOAH Splash! Did you feel that, my friend? You felt the first drop! Right on your forehead? between the eyes, as straight as a die. A perfect shot. (*Savagely*)
(MAMMA *and the children rise trembling*)

MAN Oh, you think so? Well, it was a bird — a sparrow.

NOAH And that?
(*The* MAN's *hand goes to the back of his neck*)
I suppose that was a nightingale? And that?
(*The* MAN's *hand covers his eyes*)
A robin, maybe?
(*The* MAN *stretches out his hands and quickly draws them in again*)
And those. A brace of pigeons?

MAMMA and THE CHILDREN Oh!

NOAH Dance, my friend, dance!
(*And the* MAN *dances as if he were trying to avoid a cloud of arrows*)
Shoot, O Lord! Strike this vile target, pierce it through and through!

MAMMA and THE CHILDREN (*every hand extended*) It's raining, raining, raining!
(*Pantomime of the children seeking the rain with every gesture around the man whose every gesture dodges the rain. The light is growing dim*)

NOAH Pierce the wicked eyes! The prying nose. Those ears. Seal up those lips and silence that blaspheming tongue. Pierce the hands that were never raised to You! The feet that strayed! The glutton's belly and his heart, O God, split that accursed heart. Shoot, King of Archers, shoot!
(*The* MAN *sinks down, still warding off the rain with both hands*)

MAN Help! Help! It's burning . . .
(*The light grows dimmer*)

MAMMA (*her hands stretched to the rain*) It's cool, cool like the evening breeze.

THE CHILDREN (*their hands outstretched*) Like the evening breeze.

MAMMA Like the blue of the sky.

THE CHILDREN Like the blue of the sky.

MAMMA Like the laughter of angels.

THE CHILDREN The laughter of angels. . . .

THE MAN (*on his knees*) Help me! Help me! Help me! Help me!
(*Thunder rolls*)

NOAH All aboard! Into the Ark, my good crew! Heavy weather to-night! Up into our home! Into the ship of God! You first, Mother, then you, Ada! now Sella! Naomi! Shem! Ham! Japheth! And we must sing, my children, come! all together, sing!
(*A clap of thunder*)
(*The chorus is singing in unison.* NOAH *goes up last. The storm rages. It is completely dark*)
(*The singing spreads through the Ark*)

Looking at the scene

1 List all stage directions in the scene that ask for movement. Start with

(MAMMA *and the children rise trembling*),

and end with

THE MAN (*on his knees*).

Note that all stage directions are in italic like this.

All these movements show what the man and Mamma and the children are feeling. Write down beside each direction what you think that feeling should be.

2 Is Noah in charge of this situation? How does he deal with the man? What is his relationship with God? Tell in your own words how Noah behaves.

3 Does Mamma realise what is happening? Is she working with Noah? Is she working with God? How should this part be acted?

4 Tell in two or three sentences the part played by the children.

Playreading and acting

5 Read the scene aloud in groups of nine. Think more about the words than the actions. Make sure the children speak their words together. What they say is something like music and like music it must be given at the right speed. Should that speed be slower or faster at the end when Mamma speaks and the children repeat her words?

6 Let the man and Noah in each group read the first part of the scene. Start with

NOAH Splash! Did you feel that, my friend?

and end with

MAN Help! Help! It's burning . . .

The line for Mamma and the children can be spoken by others in the group.

7 Find space for the children and the man in each group to mime the rain as it begins to fall. Follow the direction

(*Pantomime of the children seeking the rain with every gesture around the man whose every gesture dodges the rain.*)

It will probably be better if the audience sits all round the group leaving a space in the middle to perform the mime.

8 Use the same kind of space for each group to perform the complete scene.

The legend of the flood

9 The Bible story is only one of many from the Middle East that tells about an ancient flood. All of them seem to be based on an actual flood so horrific that stories about it were handed down from one generation to another. The closest story to the one in the Bible came from Babylon. Many thousands of years later (around 7 BC) it was recorded on a tablet (see the picture below) as part of a longer story called *The Epic of Gilgamesh*. Use school and public libraries to find out what you can about *The Epic of Gilgamesh* and then write a small illustrated booklet of that name.

The flood

Sheets of rain flooded the earth for forty days and forty nights. Like a waterfall from a great river the rain fell from the sky and the waters of the flood rose and rose.

Worse was to come. The beds of the seas and oceans cracked wide open and from inside the earth came great fountains and waterspouts that threw a seething mass of water towards the sky. They came together, the waterfall from the heavens and the fountains from the deep: everlasting rain falling and falling and endless water thrown up by gigantic gushers.

The water was soon deep enough for the Ark to float. It rose until even the mountains were covered and the Ark was drifting on the surface. Noah's neighbours watched it start its voyage as they were left to death by drowning in thousands of fathoms of water.

Every living thing on earth was killed: every bird, every animal and every person. On that enormous cold black flood there was nothing left under the sky. Nothing except an ark carrying eight people and some animals: enough to start life again when they came to the new world.

In this scene Mamma and the girls finally realise the extent of the flood.

Extract 3

(*Silence except for the drumming of the rain. An animal begins to howl in the hold*)

ADA   The lion's worried about something.

NAOMI   That's not the lion.

ADA   Isn't it?

NAOMI   I'd say it was the tiger.

SELLA   It isn't either of them; it's the panther. Isn't it, Mrs Noah?

MAMMA   *I* don't know, dears. All I can tell you is that it isn't the cat. Apart from the cat they all sound alike to me.
(*Laughter*)

ADA   Oh, Mrs Noah, you're sweet.
(SHEM *comes in from the rear*)

SHEM   Hello everybody. . . . It seems to be raining a bit.
(*Pause*)

MAMMA   Where are your brothers?

SHEM   Arguing. Exchanging ideas on the situation in general.

MAMMA   And father?

SHEM   He's taking a reckoning.

MAMMA   Taking a reckoning?

SHEM   That means he's trying to find out where we are.

MAMMA   What do you mean, where we are?

SHEM   What part of the world we're drifting over now.

MAMMA   Drifting? . . . Do you mean the boat is moving?

SHEM   Moving! We're tearing along.

MAMMA   What?

SHEM   Didn't you realise that?

MAMMA   I hadn't the slightest idea! (*Pause*) I . . . I thought we were floating just about our house. Yes . . . I thought all we did each day was rise a little higher above the house. . . . And — when it was all over — we'd just sink back home again.

SHEM   Oh, no. We must be at least six hundred miles away from home.

NAOMI   Really?

SHEM   Do I look as if I were joking?

SELLA   Six hundred miles!

SHEM   About! Approximately . . .
(*Silence. A howl from the hold*)

MAMMA   Then — then — we're right out at sea.

SHEM   You're quite right, Mother.

MAMMA   Good gracious me! (*She gets up*)

SHEM   What difference does that make?

MAMMA   Then, down there, underneath us — is the sea?

SHEM   Underneath us, all around us, as far as the eye can reach — all over the world.

MAMMA   And it's — it's waves that make the boat move?

SHEM   Yes, Mother, it's the salt sea waves.

MAMMA   What? Then all this water everywhere . . . is . . . *salt* water?

SHEM   I wouldn't like to swear to it. I've never tasted it, you know.

> MAMMA Is it . . . is it very deep?
>
> SHEM Incredibly deep, so father says.
> (*Silence. The beast howls. The three girls begin to cry*)
>
> MAMMA Now, now, children, you mustn't take it like this. At your age, you ought to see the bright side of things.
>
> ADA I know, but this great big ocean.
>
> NAOMI This rain —
>
> SELLA So much water!
>
> MAMMA Yes, but look at me. I always used to be so afraid of water, that during the rainy season — Noah will tell you — I didn't dare step over a puddle. And here I am in the middle of a puddle so big it hasn't any edges.
> (*Laughter*)

Looking at the scene

1 Obey cannot show the flood on a stage so he uses words to tell us what it was like. Write down the words that suggest the vastness and depth of the flood.

2 What are the feelings of Ada, Naomi and Sella after Shem has told them about the size of the flood and about what is happening to the Ark?

3 How are the sounds of the animals used to back the feelings of Mamma and the girls?

4 Why does Mamma make her little joke at the end?

5 Tell in two or three sentences how Mamma behaves.

6 What are the rest of the crew doing whilst this talking is going on? How do we know?

Setting

7 Mamma and the girls do their talking to Shem in the cabin of the Ark. Make a drawing of a stage (as you did for question 5 on page 118) to show where you would place this cabin. Tell, or draw, how a simple cabin would look and say why you have placed it in a certain area on stage.

Playreading

8 Read or act this scene in groups of six (five actors and one producer).

The legend of the flood

9 The composer Benjamin Britten set *The Deluge* (see page 131) to music and called it *Noye's Fludde*. You can hear it on a Decca/Argo ZK1 recording of the same name. Listen to the music for the storm. It is described like this:

The storm. The rain begins, and as the drops become heavier there is thunder and lightning. The waves roll and crash, the wind howls through the rigging. At the height of the storm the ark rocks wildly and the animals panic. The monkeys try to climb the rigging, a squirrel almost falls overboard, but finally Noye and his family calm the frightened animals. Above the hubbub of the storm rises the hymn Eternal Father, strong to save, *sung by Noye and all the others in the ark. Slowly the storm begins to abate.*

You may hear different movements, shapes and pictures in the music, and if so, describe what these are.

Sunshine ends the storm

Five months later a great wind blew and the terrible rain stopped. An awful silence surrounded the Ark as it floated and drifted. Then the blackness of that long dark night was pierced by the sun. The crew of the boat greeted it with a burst of joy and excitement.

Extract 4

NOAH	(*appears on deck above the cabin. Quickly the daylight brightens*) Why . . . look . . . It has stopped raining! (*The suns bursts forth*) My goodness! The sun's coming out! (*He leans over the cabin*) Children! Children, come here! (*They all rush to the bridge. The cock is crowing at the top of his lungs*) (*Quieting his flock*) Sh! Sh! Sh! On tiptoe, everybody. Walk on tiptoe. It's so fresh . . . so young . . . so delicate.
ADA	Look, the deck is steaming.
SELLA	The planks are drying up.
NAOMI	The sea is singing.
MAMMA	The silence . . .
SHEM	(*staring at the sun*) A . . . At . . . tchou!
NOAH	Sh! . . . Where's Ham?
JAPHETH	Not here, the silly ass!
NOAH	Ah well, well, well. (*Having lined them all up at the back, steps in front of them and cries in a resounding voice*) For . . . The . . . Lord . . . God! King of the Earth! (*He raises his arm*)
CHORUS	Hurray! Hurray! Hurray!
CHORUS OF ANIMALS	(*from below*) Ouahh! Ouahh! Ouahh! (*The children laugh*)
NOAH	The Golden Age! . . . Just as I said. (*A pause. He gazes at the sky, the water, the Ark, then turns to the chorus and cries profoundly joyful*) Good morning, children!
ALL	Good morning, Father!
NOAH	How are you?
ALL	Well!
NOAH	Good!
ALL	And how are *you*?
NOAH	Very well!
ALL	Splendid!
NOAH	Louder!
ALL	Splendid!
NOAH	Louder still!
ALL	Splen-did!
NOAH	That's it! We must breathe, my children, we must breathe. Like this; Ha! We must blow away these forty days of darkness, these forty nights of fear. Our lungs are choked with dust and ashes — blow them away — Ha!

ALL	Hah!
NOAH	Once again!
ALL	Hah-ah!
NOAH	There, we're washed clean. . . . I feel all new inside. In my breast — (*he taps his chest*) — there are white birds all ready to fly straight from my heart to God! . . . Oh, English is a beautiful language. . . . (*He places himself before them, his voice vibrating*) Walk, children. Let's walk! (*They line up and walk in great strides towards the audience*) To the south, as you see, we have a view of the ocean.
CHORUS	(*interested*) Aha!
NOAH	(*walking* R) To the east we have a vast expanse of water, probably salt, of an appearance and character distinctly . . . oceanic.
CHORUS	Well, well!
NOAH	(*walking up*) To the north, our prospect opens immediately on to . . . well . . . the sea.
CHORUS	How very convenient!
NOAH	Lastly, to the west we see . . . see and hear . . . the rippling laughter of the waves. (*Towards audience*) To sum up the entire situation: we are on the water.
CHORUS	We're at sea! Ha!
NOAH	Ha!
CHILDREN	Ha! Ha!
JAPHETH	Faster! (*They all walk more quickly*)
NOAH	Don't you think it's marvellous?
CHORUS	Marvellous!
JAPHETH	Faster! (*Again they quicken the pace*)
NOAH	I don't believe mother can keep up with this.
MAMMA	(*panting*) Yes . . . I can! I'm so . . . so happy.
NOAH	No, no, Mother, you needn't keep in line. Just sit out and give us your blessing.
MAMMA	(*dropping out*) Oh, Noah! You're . . . so young . . .
NOAH	Young! Upon my soul. I'm as old as the world . . . I was born . . . this morning.
CHORUS	Come on. Faster, faster!
NOAH	On the sea, beneath the sky, between the two great elements as it was in the beginning —
CHORUS	(*impatient*) Come on! Come on! Come on! Come on!
NOAH	I give up. (*He drops out and joins his wife*) But you go ahead. Go on, go on!
THE BOYS	A-Hi! . . . A-Ha! . . . Ah-Yah! Ah-You!
THE GIRLS	You-ou-ou-ou!
NOAH and MAMMA	(*sitting on the side-lines beat the measure with their hands*) March! . . . March! . . . March . . . March — march!
CHORUS	(*beside itself with joy*) Ha — ah — ah — ah . . . Ha! (*They drop down in a circle*)
ALL	The sun!!

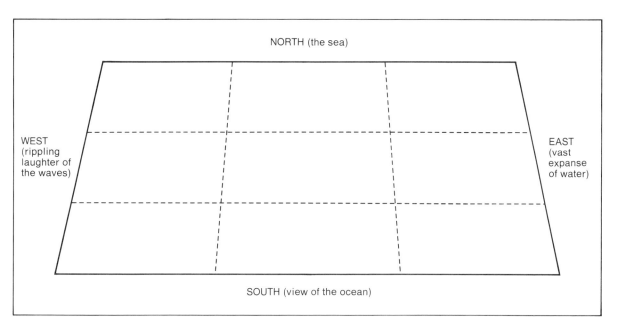

NORTH (the sea)

WEST
(rippling
laughter of
the waves)

EAST
(vast
expanse
of water)

SOUTH (view of the ocean)

Looking at the scene

1 Write out two remarks by the children that show the rain has stopped and the sun is drying out the Ark. Find two other remarks that show the deluge is over.

2 At last the children can move around after being shut up for so long. How does Noah allow them to let off steam?

3 How does Noah make fun of the fact that they are still surrounded by water as he, Mamma and the children walk around the Ark?

4 Tell in your own words how everyone is feeling. What kind of atmosphere is it?

Setting

5 Copy the drawing above of a stage. Show on your copy where Noah and the children line up before they start their walk towards the audience.

Read from the stage direction
They line up and walk in great strides towards the audience
to the end of the scene. Draw on your copy what you think is the walk on stage made by Noah and the rest of his crew.

Playreading and acting

6 Once again we have a group speaking as a chorus. Read the scene in groups of eight (seven speakers and a producer). Make sure that the group not only speaks exactly together, but also shows from the words how the crew of the Ark are feeling.

7 Find space for the same groups of eight to act in turn that part of the scene which starts with

NOAH . . . Walk, children. Let's walk!

and continues to the end.

The legend of the flood

8 Many poets have been inspired by this story. Here are ten poems which can be read aloud, acted, or used either to make illustrated poetry posters or your own anthology.

One More River (Anon) A Puffin Book of Verse
Dem Bones Gonna Rise Again (Anon) Choral Verse, Oliver and Boyd
Didn't it Rain (Anon) Junior Voices II, Penguin

127

Noah's Ark (Anon) The Penguin Book of Animal Verse

The History of the Flood (John Heath-Stubbs) The Penguin Book of Animal Verse

Noah (Roy Daniels) Themes III, Heinemann

Ballad of the Flood (Edwin Muir) Rising Early, Brockhampton

Lady Zouch (Eleanor Farjeon) Four Feet and Two, Puffin

Noah (Siegfried Sassoon) Preludes III, Heinemann

The Ballad of Mrs Noah (Robert Duncan) Modern Poetry, Oxford University Press

Drifting and dreaming

Still the Ark floated and drifted: day after day, week after week, month after month. The crew hungered for the sight of land. Then came the day. Look! What's that out there? Is it the top of a mountain? Is it land? After all this time could there still be land under all that endless water? Were the waters going down and the earth coming up?

Day by day the water level fell, and little by little the earth was uncovered. The peaks of mountains rose slowly out of the water and the Ark drifted helplessly between them. So many questions needed to be answered. Was there life on that mountain peak? Was the earth dry enough for everyone to leave the Ark?

Noah decided to send a dove to find out. If it returned then everything would be all right, if it did not their stay on the Ark would continue. The crew held their breath as the dove whirred in a straight line farther and farther away until it was out of sight.

Extract 5

NOAH	. . . Ada, my child, you are the youngest here. Go and fetch the little white-winged creature, the purest and loveliest of all the animals. Go and fetch the dove.
CHORUS	The dove?
NOAH	Yes, the dove.
NAOMI	Hm! Hm!
CHORUS	Sh!
HAM	You'll spoil the effect.
NAOMI	I'm so excited!

CHORUS Sh!

(ADA *returns with the dove*)

NOAH No, no, dear, let it go yourself.

ADA Oh, I'm not —

NOAH Just let it go like that, quite easily.

ADA No, no, Mr Noah, I daren't.

NOAH Very well, then, give it to me. (*He takes the bird from* ADA's *hands*)

ALL Let it go, let it go!

NOAH Tell me, children, don't you think a nice little prayer would fit into the picture?

ALL Later, later!

NOAH (*laughing*) Well, well, what a patient family I've got to be sure. All right, then. . . . One, two, three . . . Go!

ALL Go!

(*Silence. Every head is thrown back, watching the flight of the dove in three great circles*)

Good-bye! Good-bye!

JAPHETH Look how she's climbing!

SELLA The wind's carrying her right up to the sky!

ALL Yes, yes, straight up!

HAM Straight into God's mouth.

NOAH Ssh! Ssh!

SHEM	'Ware below! The wind's knocking her down! She's falling!
ALL	Falling!
JAPHETH	No, no, no! She's up again!
NOAH	Bravo, little one. Look at her! Look how she's climbing! Climbing the snow-caps, higher and higher, into the distant blue. Bravo, my brave little mountaineer!
SELLA	I can't see her any more.
ALL	Neither can we.
HAM	Perhaps God's eaten her.
ALL	No, no, no, no. We won't listen.
ADA	There she is again!
ALL	Where? Where?
ADA	There where I'm pointing. . . . Higher! Much higher! . . . See that cloud like a horse's head? Well, just beyond that!
ALL	Oh yes!
	(*For a little time everyone gazes up into space*)
MAMMA	I can't see her any more. I'm feeling dizzy. There are spots in front of my eyes.
JAPHETH	Now I've lost her myself.
ALL	So have we. We've lost it.
NOAH	She's disappeared.
ALL	(*gently*) Oh! . . .

Looking at the scene

1 Why is everyone so excited about releasing the dove?

2 Where in the scene is there a pause for stillness?

3 How does the behaviour of Ham differ from that of the others?

4 What is the mood of everyone at the end?

5 Here is a short description of Mamma:

> Mrs Noah does her best to make the Ark into a home. She stays in the background offering support and comfort to her husband and acts as a good mother to her grown sons and their girl friends.

Describe in the same way any *two* of the other characters in the play.

Setting

6 Show with a simple diagram how you would group the eight actors on the deck of the Ark in order to act this scene.

Playreading and acting

7 Form groups of nine (eight speakers and a producer) to read and act this extract. There is no dove, of course, so you will need to concentrate hard on the flight of an imaginary bird in order to make others believe in it.

The legend of the flood

8 This story of the flood has given us several expressions which we still use today, e.g.

- You must have come out of the Ark (because you are so old-fashioned)
- Why not hold out an olive branch? (make signs of peace)

The French have similar sayings such as *après nous le déluge* which means roughly 'let's enjoy ourselves now and not worry about the future'.

How many other sayings can you find which are connected with the flood, the Ark, the dove, the olive branch and the rainbow? What do they mean?

Mutiny!

The eight people had been shut up together for months now and there was trouble on the Ark. The children were bored, restless and discontented, and the long, long voyage had been very hard and trying for them. War broke out between them and Noah: between youth and age. Ham emerged as their leader, with ideas of his own, a rebel who disagreed with his father and all he stood for.

A powerful wind was blowing and Ham urged the others to put up a mast and a sail so that they might steer the boat wherever they wanted. The mountain peaks could be avoided and the Ark brought safely to land at a place that had escaped the flood. No longer was the boat to be in God's hands: the children were to take command. The old man was wrong and his old-fashioned ideas were not working out. There had to be change.

Extract 6

HAM   (*to* NOAH) We don't believe you any longer. We don't believe the pretty fairy tales that drop from heaven.

THE CHILDREN   No, we don't!

HAM   We only believe in the truth that we know ourselves.

THE CHILDREN   That's right! That's what we believe!

HAM   We want to live! We want excitement and adventure. We want to make discoveries and risk dangers. What's the good of humility and prayer and contemplation — that's all just cowardly laziness. We want to live!

THE CHILDREN   That's what we want!

HAM   Forward! Forward! Set up the mast! Hoist the sail — our fine big sail. We'll catch this wind and head straight for the south, rolling with the ship, singing with the ship, laughing as we know how to laugh!

THE CHILDREN   Hahaha! Come on, come on!
(*They break into chant, and rush away to get the mast and the sail.* MAMMA *remains alone*)

NOAH   And where do you think you are going, you young fool?

HAM   Somewhere there must be land — cities — people — crowds of people — that never saw your flood! All over the world there are men who won't even believe all this when we tell it.

NOAH   That's not true.

HAM   I know it is!

NOAH   It's not true! It's not true!

HAM   It is true! I feel it! We all feel it! Come on, forward!

THE CHILDREN   (*returning*) Forward! Forward!
(*They raise the mast, singing*)

NOAH   You can't! You can't! It's wicked!

HAM   I'll take the blame.

THE CHILDREN   So will we!
(*The mast rises*)

Looking at the scene

1 What new view of life do the children now have?

2 Answer 'a' and 'b' below after looking at the speech by Ham that starts with 'We want to live!'
   a How do the children intend to find the excitement and adventure they want?
   b What three things mentioned by Ham show Noah's way of life?

3 Which of the lines in the scene tells us that Noah's advice will not be taken?

4 Why does Noah think that the raising of the mast is wicked?

5 Tell in your own words how Ham feels about Noah at this stage.

6 Look again at the opening of the play on page 116. Does it hold your attention and make you keen to know what happens next? What kind of an opening is it? Tell whether or not you think it makes a good start to the play.

Setting

7 Describe, or show by a drawing, how on stage you would raise the mast safely.

8 Should the mast be raised on the Ark itself, which is stage right, or centre stage with the Ark shut off from the audience? Give reasons for your decision.

Playreading and acting

9 Form groups of nine (eight actors and a producer) to perform this scene. In it we have the children showing their feelings in movement and song. They are excited and, after defying Noah, sing as they rush away to get the mast and the sail. There is more singing on their return, for with the mast raised high it is now ready to take them to adventure and danger. Sea shanties such as *Blow the man down* might be suitable songs to sing.

The legend of the flood

10 The story of Noah was popular during the Middle Ages and was often performed as a play called *The Deluge* by the water drawers and water carriers of the River Dee in Chester. Find out what you can about the Chester pageant of *The Deluge* and how and why this medieval mystery play was performed.

Good old earth

A whirr of wings brought the rebellion to a halt. The dove had returned! Its beak held a green twig on which there were three little leaves: three leaves from an olive tree. Somewhere on earth life had returned and trees were once again growing.

It seemed safe to leave the home that had carried them safely through the flood, and the children were the first to go. After months of being cooped up there was now room to move around, to see something new, and to feel the earth again. They rushed about for joy on the newly revealed earth.

Extract 7

ALL	Ah!
THE BOYS	Aha!
THE GIRLS	Haha!
	(*They are all lined up before the Ark*)
HAM	Ha! Old Earth!
THE BOYS	Good old Earth!
THE GIRLS	Dear old Earth!
JAPHETH	(*stepping out of line*) Look! I'm going to walk! Watch me walk! (*He takes a step*) What am I doing?
ALL	Walking!
JAPHETH	(*slapping his chest*) What's this boy doing?
ALL	He's walking!
JAPHETH	Walking where?
ALL	On the ground!
NAOMI	(*getting out of line*) Look at me! Look at me! (*She pulls her skirts up to her knees*)
ADA and SELLA	(*copying her*) Look at us.
NAOMI	(*tapping the ground*) I'm squelching in the mud.
ADA and SELLA	We're squelching, too.
THE BOYS	Let's all squelch. (*They do so*)
HAM	It's wet!
JAPHETH	It's cold!
SHEM	But it's warming up under our feet.
THE THREE BOYS	It's soft! It feels so good!
ALL	One, two! One, two!
NAOMI	(*with a shrill laugh*) Look! My feet are all black!
ALL	One, two! One, two!
HAM	(*getting out of line*) Be quiet!
ALL	One, two!
HAM	Shut up! Shut up! (*Pause*) I want to feel that at last — I'm really *free*!

Looking at the scene

1 The words here are so simple they read just like those in a book for very young children. Obey uses such simple language in order to show us either (a) that these are children talking, or (b) the feelings of the characters. Is it (a) or (b) that is right? Give your reasons.

2 Look at the language again. Nobody in real life would ever talk like this so why is it done here?

3 If you were acting the part of one of the children how would you say the words 'Good old Earth' and 'Dear old Earth'? Remember that you have not seen the earth for many months and at one time thought you would never do so again.

4 Describe an action you might use to go with the words 'Good old Earth' and 'Dear old Earth'.

5 The boys and girls are squelching about in the mud like four-year-olds when Ham steps out of line to shout at them. Why does he do this and what does it tell us about his character?

6 Make a drawing of a stage and show on it the boys and girls lined up before the Ark (use small circles containing the first letter of each name). Read the stage directions and then show on your drawing the movement as each one steps out of line to form a *different* pattern as they squelch in the mud.

Setting

7 Draw or describe the set for this scene. The front of the Ark will just be seen at the right side but where will you place the mound of earth and any vegetation?

8 Solve the problem of the return of the dove to the Ark if a real bird cannot be used on stage.

Acting

9 Form groups of seven (six actors and a producer) to act this piece. Remember that the six boys and girls have to show what it feels like to be on land again, that they will be unsteady on their legs after the long voyage, and that the acting area will have no mud on it.

The world begins again

Such joy did not last for long. Soon the boys were quarrelling and fighting one another in order to prove who was the leader.

Suddenly they were pushed aside as the animals poured from the Ark. Galloping, leaping and thundering they rushed for the goodness of the earth they needed. As they scattered down the mountain, with the birds winging above them, the children at first watched and then set off to follow.

Ham and Naomi went southwards, Shem and Sella to the east, and Japheth and Ada westwards. They were to found the great races of earth: the black, the yellow and the white.

The world had begun again.

Extract 8

HAM	(*from his height*) Ham is on top of his world.
JAPHETH	(*climbing up*) Here comes Japheth.
HAM	No, you don't.
SHEM	Shem's coming too!
HAM	Neither Japheth *nor* Shem! (*Planting himself firmly, he keeps them off with both hands*)
NAOMI	(*upstage*) We're on a mountain.
SELLA and ADA	A high mountain.

Mt Ararat

(*The three girls separate.* SELLA *goes down* R, ADA *up* C, NAOMI *down* L. *Meanwhile* SHEM *and* JAPHETH *shout and attack the hill from opposite sides*)

HAM (*driving them off*) No! No! No, you don't.

SHEM and JAPHETH (*slipping*) Why not?

HAM I climbed up first. I got here first! I'm the strongest.

SHEM I'm the oldest.

JAPHETH Well, I'm the youngest.

(*They come to blows.* NOAH *turns and watches without saying anything*)

ADA Look at the water! It's streaming down the mountain in little rills.

SELLA The animals are streaming down after them.

NAOMI Everything's streaming down. They're all going down.

ADA There are plains already.

SELLA There's a jungle, too.

NAOMI And deserts, too.

(*The boys are fighting*)

THE GIRLS (*running toward them*) No!

JAPHETH (*to* HAM) Black man! Blackamoor! Nigger!

SHEM (*to* JAPHETH) Baby! Cissy! Pale face!

HAM (*to* SHEM) Yellow! Yellow skin! Chink!

(*They roll down the hill and start up again. But their wives cling to them*)

NAOMI No, no! Why fight over a little lump of rock when the world is so wide.

SELLA The world is all around us.

ADA There it is! Down there!

THE THREE GIRLS Down there! Down there!

(*But the boys free themselves and go back to their fight*)

JAPHETH (*to* SHEM). Chink! Slant-eyes!

HAM (*to* JAPHETH) Pale face! Whitey!

SHEM (*to* HAM) Nigger. Blackamoor!

(*They roll down the hill again. The girls pick them up and hold them fast*)

NAOMI (*to* HAM) Behind you, Ham! Look behind you. Southward. Southward! Look straight into the south. Come. Come, my hunter. Follow the lion over the sands to the south!

SELLA (*to* SHEM) To the East! To the East! After the tiger! We'll ride on elephant through the jungle, where monkeys chatter as we pass. Come, my peasant!

ADA (*to* JAPHETH) Come, my shepherd. Take up your pipes. We'll follow the cow and the sheep and the dog into the mists and valleys of the west. Come, my shepherd!

(*The three panting boys each turns in his own direction*)

THE GIRLS Come!

NAOMI All life has gone down the mountain.

(*The boys start to follow the girls, then suddenly turn and embrace*)

THE BOYS Good-bye!

THE GIRLS Come!

(*They run and gather up their bundles.* NAOMI *struggles up with hers and* HAM'S *and puts them on her head.* SHEM *loads his on his shoulder.* JAPHETH *and* ADA *put theirs together and carry them between them*)

Looking at the scene

1 Why are the boys fighting?
2 What is seen by the girls when they turn their backs on the boys and go to different sides of the mountain top?
3 We now learn that each of the boys belongs to one of the three great races of the world: the black, the yellow and the white. To which race does each belong?
4 a What argument do the girls offer to stop the boys fighting?
   b How is the fighting finally stopped?
5 To which part of the world is each couple going? Where, earlier in the scene, is there a suggestion of this?
6 What are the three jobs the girls see the boys doing?
7 What part does Noah play in this scene?
8 Describe your favourite scene from *Noah* and say why you like it.

Acting

9 Form groups of seven (three boys, three girls and a producer) to act this scene. The main problems are the mountain (boxes with a cloth over them?) and the fight sequences. Some thought should be given to both of these. It is also important that stage directions be followed very carefully.

The legend of the flood

10 The Bible says that the Ark came to rest on one of the mountains in the country of Ararat (Urartu) in eastern Turkey. Mt Ararat has been climbed many times in recent years by people (including an American astronaut) looking for the remains of the Ark but nothing has yet been found.

Use school and public libraries to find Mt Ararat on an atlas and draw a rough map to show its position. If you are interested, add other information about Mt Ararat and the quest for the lost Ark.

God's promise to Noah

With both the children and his old friends the wild animals gone, Noah is left alone with Mrs Noah.

The play ends as it starts, with Noah talking to God. He asks that now and then he be given an assurance that everything is all right, and that he will not have to go through that experience again. God gives Noah the sign he seeks, a rainbow in seven heavenly colours. He also makes this promise:

Never again will I put the earth under a curse because of what man does . . .
Never again will I destroy all living beings, as I have done this time.
As long as the world exists, there will be a time for planting and a time for harvest. There will always be cold and heat, summer and winter, day and night.

Genesis 8

Extract 9

NOAH It's a good thing I have such trust in You. . . . Do You hear? I'll say You've given me some pretty hard knocks. It's been a bit past a joke sometimes, I can tell You! You take me from my garden and chuck me on a bare rock, all by myself, with a hundred ways of dying. . . . Haha! . . . All right, all right. Don't You worry. I'll find a way out, somehow or other. I'll find a way out all right! I tell You frankly I've given up trying to understand. But no matter. Go on, I'm following you! Oh, let's go on! Only just one thing I'd like to ask You. Be up there a bit just now and again, will You? Just let me hear Your voice once in a while, or feel Your breath, just see Your light, even. Lord, if You'd just shed Your light on my work as I do it every day, and give the *feeling — the assurance —* the conviction that You are satisfied. We must all be satisfied, mustn't we? (*He attacks the Ark with his hatchet*) Well, I am satisfied. (*He shouts*) I am satisfied! (*He sings*) Are You satisfied!

(*The seven colours of the rainbow appear in the background*)
That's fine!

CURTAIN.

Curtain call

1 Write out the sentence that shows Noah now feels he can manage for himself.
2 What is the assurance given by God to Noah?
3 Noah has now finished with the Ark. Which stage direction indicates this?
4 Write a sentence or two telling how Noah talks to God. Is it different in any way to his speech in the opening scene?
5 Make *three* statements about Shem and illustrate each one with an example, e.g.

  Statement: Shem is the oldest of the three boys.
  Illustration: He says this when the boys are quarrelling after the Ark has come to rest.

6 Make a statement about each of the girls and illustrate it with an example.
7 Make *three* statements about Japheth and illustrate each one with an example.
8 Describe in your own words the most *dramatic* scene from *Noah.*
9 When does Mamma show her qualities as a wife and when as a mother?
10 Does the play have a moral for you? What is the moral? Give your reasons.
11 Does *Noah* have anything to say about our own time? Has the world become so violent and evil that it ought to be destroyed and a fresh start made? Say what you think in a paragraph or two.
12 Write a story, or a short play, about a second destruction of the earth. Include a spaceship called *The Ark* in which there is a crew, plants and animals, waiting for a time to land safely.

Poetry

Poetry

The following are two descriptions of an eagle. The passage of prose is taken from a book describing the habits of birds, and the second is a short poem about the eagle.

Read them both closely a number of times and look for the differences not only in what each writer says but in the way it is said.

Eagles are usually first seen soaring over the hillside or perhaps perching in silhouette on the skyline. When they change from soaring to flapping flight the beats look slow and heavy, but, in fact, they can travel very fast. When hunting, they search the ground carefully, then swoop to grip the prey in their talons. They take hares, rabbits, grouse and other birds, and sometimes small lambs; and they have been known to attack young deer; they also eat carrion. Fights with wild cats have been recorded, but they are not usually courageous birds, even in defence of their nests. They are clumsy walkers, rolling from side to side.

The Oxford Book of Birds

He clasps the crag with crooked hands;
Close to the sun in lonely lands,
Ring'd with the azure world, he stands.

The wrinkled sea beneath him crawls;
He watches from his mountain walls,
And like a thunderbolt he falls.

Alfred, Lord Tennyson

The following are some of the obvious differences.

1 The poem is divided into lines; each line is of a certain length. Count the number of syllables in each line of the poem.

2 *RHYME*   The lines in the poem end in words which *rhyme* — hands, lands, stands; crawls, walls, falls. Not all poems rhyme, but when rhyme is used it draws together the lines. Rhyme is of importance in most humorous verse and often there is a number of different syllables rhyming, e.g. funny 'un, bunion.

3 *RHYTHM*   The syllables form a pattern in the lines of the poem. Repeat them a number of times and you will find that every second syllable has a strong emphasis, accent, or beat. This pattern is called *rhythm* and is the main difference between prose and poetry. The rhythm of a poem is important in helping you to feel the atmosphere or appreciate the description; that is why advertisers on TV often use strong rhythms and why you hear chanting at football matches.

Other points often present in poetry

As poets have to make a point with as few words as possible, they tend to cram as much meaning into each word as they can.

4 *The Sound of Words*
   Say the first line of the poem a number of times.
   What sound is repeated?
   Is it a soft, hard, or smooth sound?
   What does it suggest?

5 Good poems often appeal to the imagination. The passage of prose gives us a series of facts about the eagle. The poem also gives us some of these facts but in such a way as to appeal to our imagination. Writers often use similes and metaphors to describe as vividly as possible.

6 A *SIMILE* is a direct comparison introduced by the words 'like' or 'as'; e.g.
   And like a thunderbolt he falls.
   The speed of the eagle swooping on to his victim is compared to the speed of a thunderbolt coming out of the sky. What other things do you associate with a thunderbolt? Do they also apply to the eagle?

If a simile is able to suggest a number of things at once then it is a very rich, vivid comparison.

7 A *METAPHOR* is a type of comparison but instead of saying one thing is like another, in a metaphor we describe or refer to the first thing in terms of the other; e.g.

The wrinkled sea beneath him crawls.

Here the sea is being described in terms of a face with wrinkles. What else does it suggest about the sea and the waves? Are they rough or calm? If you think about it carefully you will find that the poet is describing the sea from the point of view of the height of the eagle.

In the first three lines, however, he seems to be looking up from below at the eagle. Which metaphors suggest this?

What does the word 'crawls' suggest to you? In what way can you say that the sea crawls?

Like similes, good metaphors appeal to the imagination and suggest many points of comparison which we could easily overlook. We are using metaphors all the time in our language, and we have to be sometimes careful that we realise they are metaphors. For instance, how do you think a foreigner would react if he asked the quickest way to London and was given the following answer?

'Go straight across the first traffic island and then pick up the M6.'

Or what would he think if he read in a report of a football match.

'Williams raced down the wing, crossed a beautiful square ball to Rodgers, who bent it round the goalkeeper'?

Exercises

1 He was as fast as a gazelle. He was as fast as a leopard.
a What is the point of comparison in both of these sentences?
b What does the different choice of the comparisons suggest in addition?
c Suggest other comparisons (similes) with people and animals.

2 Point out which words are metaphors in the following and say what they suggest.
a The green field sleeps in the sun.
b Although there is a sugary smile on his face, there was a poisonous look in his eyes.
c The moon was a ghostly galleon tossed upon cloudy seas.

3 Repeat the following a number of times out loud and say what the sound of the words suggests to you.
a The murmur of innumerable bees among summer elms.
b The silvery snakes slide through the grass.
c The great bell boomed and clanged across the silence of the seas.
d The creaking, groaning gate swings on rusty hinges.
e Lilies that fester smell far worse than weeds.
f The gondola glides through smooth, moving waters.

Light verse and humour

School Report

'Too easily satisfied. Spelling still poor.
  Her grammar's erratic. Lacks care.
Would succeed if she worked. Inclined to be smug.'
  I think that's a wee bit unfare.

Ah well, their it is! Disappointing perhaps,
  For a mum what has always had brane,
But we can't all have looks or be good at our books . . .
  She's her father all over agane.

Carole Paine

Roast Swan Song

Aforetime, by the waters wan,
This lovely body I put on:
In life I was a stately swan.

Ah me! Ah me!
5 *Now browned and basted thoroughly.*

The cook now turns me round and turns me.
The hurrying waiter next concerns me,
But oh, this fire, how fierce it burns me!

Ah me! Ah me!

10 Would I might glide, my plumage fluffing,
On pools to feel the cool wind soughing,
Rather than burst with pepper-stuffing.

Ah me! Ah me!

Once I was whiter than the snow,
15 The fairest bird that earth could show;
Now I am blacker than the crow.

Ah me! Ah me!

Here I am dished upon the platter.
I cannot fly. Oh, what's the matter?
20 Lights flash, teeth clash — I fear the latter.

Ouch! . . . Ouch! . . .   Anon,   tr. George F Whicher

The Fate of the Supermarket Manager

There once was a Supermarket manager
And a very happy manager was he.

He *reduced the prices*
Of the lollies and the ices!
5   He made *huge cuts*
On the fruit and nuts!
Corn-flakes, steaks
And home-bake cakes,
Dog-food, detergent,
10   Devil-fish, dates,
He sold at *half*
The market rates!
And (so my sister
Said to me)
15   He put stickers
On the knickers
In the Lingerie
Saying:
Prices down
20   By 15p!
And he wrote, as a treat,
By the luncheon meat:
YOU'D HAVE TO BE BARMY
TO BUY THIS SALAMI
25   So he gave it away
For free!

Yes, there once was a Supermarket manager
And a very happy manager was he.

What a bloke!

30   He was much admired.

The shop went broke.

He was fired.

Kit Wright

The National Union of Children

NUC has just passed a weighty resolution:
'Unless all parents raise our rate of pay
This action will be taken by our members
(The resolution comes in force today): —

'Noses will not be blown (sniffs are in order),
Bedtime will get preposterously late,
Ice-cream and crisps will be consumed for breakfast,
Unwanted cabbage left upon the plate,

'Earholes and fingernails can't be inspected,
Overtime (known as homework) won't be worked,
Reports from school will all say "Could do better",
Putting bricks back in boxes may be shirked.'

Roy Fuller

Horrible Things

'What's the horriblest thing you've seen?'
Said Nell to Jean.

'Some grey-coloured, trodden-on Plasticine;
On a plate, a left-over cold baked bean;
A cloak-room ticket numbered thirteen;
A slice of meat without any lean;
The smile of a spiteful fairy-tale queen;
A thing in the sea like a brown submarine;
A cheese fur-coated in brilliant green;
A bluebottle perched on a piece of sardine.
What's the horriblest thing YOU'VE seen?'
Said Jean to Nell.

'Your face as you tell
Of all the horriblest things you've seen.'

Roy Fuller

Telling a story

A story has a setting, characters and actions, but these do not always play an equal part in the story. Sometimes the action is only suggested and you have to guess what it is (e.g. *What Has Happened to Lulu?*) and the same can apply to the characters (e.g. *Who?*).

In other stories the main interest lies in what happens and the way it is described (e.g. *The Lion and Albert*). Look at all the following narrative poems and decide what part the settings, characters and actions play.

At a Country Fair

At a bygone Western country fair
I saw a giant led by a dwarf
With a red string like a long thin scarf;
How much he was the stronger there
5   The giant seemed unaware.

And then I saw that the giant was blind,
And the dwarf a shrewd-eyed little thing;
The giant, mild, timid, obeyed the string
As if he had no independent mind,
10   Or will of any kind.

Wherever the dwarf decided to go
At his heels the other trotted meekly,
(Perhaps — I know not — reproaching weakly)
Like one Fate bade that it must be so,
15   Whether he wished or no.

Various sights in various climes
I have seen, and more I may see yet,
But that sight never shall I forget,
And have thought it the sorriest of pantomimes,
20   If once, a hundred times!

Thomas Hardy

1 Describe the scene as the poet saw it.
2 What were the poet's feelings about what he saw?
3 How does the setting increase your sympathy for the giant?
4 Pick out the words which best describe:
a the dwarf,
b the giant's manner.
Pick out pairs of words that contrast.
5 What is puzzling about the scene?
6 Although there is a setting and characters there is little action and yet a lot of action is implied. Make up a story explaining how the situation came about.
7 Try to describe either in a poem or prose and bringing out contrast and sympathy for the subjects:
a a mother animal and her young
b a once famous sports star now poor or disabled
c a group of old soldiers
8 The following have been exhibited at fairs and holiday resorts. Do you think it right that they should be?
a a two-headed sheep
b the fattest woman in the world
c Siamese twins

The Lion and Albert

There's a famous seaside place called Blackpool,
   That's noted for fresh air and fun,
And Mr and Mrs Ramsbottom
   Went there with young Albert, their son.

5 A grand little lad was young Albert,
   All dressed in his best; quite a swell
With a stick with an 'orse's 'ead 'andle,
   The finest that Woolworth's could sell.

They didn't think much to the Ocean:
10   The waves, they was fiddlin' and small,
There was no wrecks and nobody drownded,
   Fact, nothing to laugh at at all.

So, seeking for further amusement,
   They paid and went into the Zoo,
15 Where they'd Lions and Tigers and Camels,
   And old ale and sandwiches too.

There were one great big Lion called Wallace;
   His nose were all covered with scars —
He lay in a somnolent posture,
20   With the side of his face on the bars.

Now Albert had heard about Lions,
   How they was ferocious and wild —
To see Wallace lying so peaceful,
   Well, it didn't seem right to the child.

25 So straightway the brave little feller,
   Not showing a morsel of fear,
Took his stick with its 'orse's 'ead 'andle
   And pushed it in Wallace's ear.

You could see that the Lion didn't like it,
30   For giving a kind of a roll,
He pulled Albert inside the cage with 'im,
   And swallowed the little lad 'ole.

Then Pa, who had seen the occurrence,
   And didn't know what to do next,
35 Said 'Mother! Yon Lion's 'et Albert',
   And Mother said 'Well, I am vexed!'

Then Mr and Mrs Ramsbottom —
   Quite rightly, when all's said and done —
Complained to the Animal Keeper,
40   That the Lion had eaten their son.

The keeper was quite nice about it;
   He said 'What a nasty mishap.
Are you sure that it's *your* boy he's eaten?'
   Pa said 'Am I sure? There's his cap!'

45   The manager had to be sent for.
   He came and he said 'What's to do?'
Pa said 'Yon Lion's 'et Albert,
   And 'im in his Sunday clothes, too.'

Then Mother said, 'Right's right, young feller;
50   I think it's a shame and a sin,
For a lion to go and eat Albert,
   And after we've paid to come in.'

The manager wanted no trouble,
   He took out his purse right away,
55 Saying 'How much to settle the matter?'
   And Pa said 'What do you usually pay?'

But Mother had turned a bit awkward
   When she thought where her Albert had gone.
She said 'No! someone's got to be summonsed' —
60   So that was decided upon.

Then off they went to the P'lice Station,
   In front of the Magistrate chap;
They told 'im what happened to Albert,
   And proved it by showing his cap.

65   The Magistrate gave his opinion
   That no one was really to blame
And he said that he hoped the Ramsbottoms
   Would have further sons to their name.

At that Mother got proper blazing,
70   'And thank you, sir, kindly,' said she.
'What waste all our lives raising children
   To feed ruddy Lions? Not me!'

Marriott Edgar

The North Ship

Legend

I saw three ships go sailing by,
Over the sea, the lifting sea,
And the wind rose in the morning sky,
And one was rigged for a long journey.

5 The first ship turned towards the west,
Over the sea, the running sea,
And by the wind was all possessed
And carried to a rich country.

The second turned towards the east,
10 Over the sea, the quaking sea,
And the wind hunted it like a beast
To anchor in captivity.

The third ship drove towards the north,
Over the sea, the darkening sea,
15 But no breath of wind came forth,
And the decks shone frostily.

The northern sky rose high and black
Over the proud unfruitful sea,
East and west the ships came back
20 Happily or unhappily:

But the third went wide and far
Into an unforgiving sea
Under a fire-spilling star,
And it was rigged for a long journey.

Philip Larkin

What Has Happened to Lulu?

What has happened to Lulu, mother?
  What has happened to Lu?
There's nothing in her bed but an old rag doll
  And by its side a shoe.

5 Why is her window wide, mother,
  The curtain flapping free,
And only a circle on the dusty shelf
  Where her money-box used to be?

Why do you turn your head, mother,
10 And why do the tear-drops fall?
And why do you crumple that note on the fire
  And say it is nothing at all?

I woke to voices late last night,
  I heard an engine roar.
15 Why do you tell me the things I heard
  Were a dream and nothing more?

I heard somebody cry, mother,
  In anger or in pain,
But now I ask you why, mother,
20 You say it was a gust of rain.

Why do you wander about as though
  You don't know what to do?
What has happened to Lulu, mother?
  What has happened to Lu?

Charles Causley

A Close Encounter

I was returning from a friend's one night
when our street was bathed in a ghostly light
and an eerie drone filled the air.

My trembling hand clutched the gate, and there —
5 in the middle of the road — large and round
was a shining object touching down.

It shimmered and glowed as if alive;
made a humming and buzzing as if a hive
of bees was swarming inside.

10 Well, I tell you this and I swear it's no lie;
a trapdoor opened, a ladder swung down
and a strange looking creature wobbled down to the ground.

Its huge nodding head was a great bulbous dome.
It had one staring eye in a forehead of chrome
15 and it was looking straight at me!

Then it lifted up its lobster claw
and beckoned me gently to its door
slowly shifting its grasshopper legs.

It had no mouth but it made a noise
20 which must have come from a hidden voice.
Its electric crackle plainly said:

'We have come from Mars the planet red.
We offer peace and friendship to every man
You are welcome to visit our land, if you can.

25 Step inside, earthling. Do not be afraid.
We have ideas to exchange and thoughts to trade.
There is much to be learnt from each other.'

Though I knew the words he spoke were true,
I was much too frightened to know what to do.
30 So I fled up the path to our house.

A welcoming light, and my mum making toast.
'What on earth can be wrong?' said my dad.
'Have you just seen a ghost?'

Adrian Rumble

Who?

Who is that child I see wandering, wandering
Down by the side of the quivering stream?
Why does he seem not to hear, though I call to him?
Where does he come from, and what is his name?

5 Why do I see him at sunrise and sunset
Taking, in old-fashioned clothes, the same track?
Why, when he walks, does he cast not a shadow
Though the sun rises and falls at his back?

Why does the dust lie so thick on the hedgerow
10 By the great field where a horse pulls the plough?
Why do I see only meadows, where houses
Stand in a line by the riverside now?

Why does he move like a wraith by the water,
Soft as the thistledown on the breeze blown?
15 When I draw near him so that I may hear him,
Why does he say that his name is my own?

Charles Causley

151

One of our St Bernard Dogs is Missing

A moot point
Whether I was going to
Make it.
I just had the strength
5 To ring the bell.

There were monks inside
And one of them
Eventually
Opened the door.
10 Oh
He said,
This is a bit of a turn-up
He said
For the book.
15 Opportune
He said
Your arriving at this particular
As it were
Moment

20 You're dead right
I said
It was touch and go
Whether I could have managed
To keep going
25 For very much
Longer.

No
He said
The reason I used the word opportune
30 Is that
Not to put too fine a point on it
One of our St Bernard dogs is
Unfortunately
Missing.

35 Oh, dear
I said.
Not looking for me, I hope.

No
He said.
40 It went for a walk
And got lost in the snow.

Dreadful thing
I said
To happen.

45 Yes
He said.
It is.

To
Of all creatures
50 I said
A St Bernard dog
That has devoted
Its entire
Life
55 To doing good
And helping
Others.

What I was actually thinking
He said
60 Since you happen to be
In a manner of speaking
Out there already
Is that
If you could
65 At all
See your way clear
To having a scout
As it were
Around,
70 It would save one of us

Having to
If I can so put it
Turn out.
Ah
75 I said
That would
I suppose
Make a kind of sense.

80 Before you go
    He said
    If I can find it
    You'd better
    Here it is
85 Take this.

    What is it?
    I said
    It's a flask
    He said
90 Of brandy.
    Ah
    I said.

    For the dog
    He said.

    Good thinking
95 I said.

    The drill
    He said
    When you find it
    If you ever do
100 Is to lie down.

    Right
    I said
    Will do.

    Lie down on top of it
105 He said
    To keep it warm
    Till help arrives.

    That was a week ago, and my hopes are rising all the time.
    I feel with ever-increasing confidence
110 that once I can safely say that I am within what might
    be called striking distance of knowing where, within a
    square mile or two, to start getting down to looking,
    my troubles are more or less, to all intents and
    purposes, apart from frostbite, with any luck once
115 help arrives at long last, God willing, as good as over.
    It is good to be spurred on with hope.

                                    N F Simpson

Thinking things over

The Fringe of the Sea

We do not like to awaken
far from the fringe of the sea,
we who live upon small islands.

We like to rise up early,
5   quick in the agile mornings
and walk out only little distances
to look down at the water,

to know it is swaying near to us
with songs, and tides, and endless boatways,
10   and undulate patterns and moods.

We want to be able to saunter beside it
slowpaced in burning sunlight,
barearmed, barefoot, bareheaded,

and to stoop down by the shallows
15   sifting the random water
between assaying fingers
like farmers do with soil,

and to think of turquoise mackerel
turning with consummate grace,
20   sleek and decorous
and elegant in high blue chambers.

We want to be able to walk out into it,
to work in it,
dive and swim and play in it,

25   to row and sail
and pilot over its sandless highways,
and to hear
its call and murmurs wherever we may be.

All who have lived upon small islands
30   want to sleep and awaken
close to the fringe of the sea.

A. L. Hendriks

1 Read aloud lines 8 to 10 two or three times.
a What is the main sound used in the lines?
b How does it fit in with the description?
c Find other parts of the poem where the same effect is created.

2 Read lines 25 to 28 out aloud two or three times. Which of the following words best describes the rhythm?

swaying   marching   jerky

Give reasons for your choice.

3 Point out three aspects of living near the sea that the writer enjoys.

4 Point out the lines in which you think the writer has been particularly successful in making living on a sunny island sound attractive.

5 What do you think the writer means by the following word pictures?
a agile mornings
b elegant in high blue chambers
c sandless highways

6 Write a short paragraph describing in your own words:
a the roar of the sea
b waves lapping on the shore during the night

7 Would you like to live on a small island in a sunny climate? Describe what you imagine a holiday there would be like.

8 What difficulties do you think that people brought up on a small sunny island would find if they came to live in a city in Britain?

Why Nobody Pets the Lion at the Zoo

The morning that the world began
The Lion growled a growl at Man.

And I suspect the Lion might
(If he'd been closer) have tried a bite.

5 I think that's as it ought to be
And not as it was taught to me.

I think the Lion has a right
To growl a growl and bite a bite.

And if the Lion bothered Adam,
10 He should have growled right back at 'im.

The way to treat a Lion right
Is growl for growl and bite for bite.

True, the Lion is better fit
For biting than for being bit.

15 But if you look him in the eye
You'll find the Lion's rather shy.

He really wants someone to pet him.
The trouble is: his teeth won't let him.

He has a heart of gold beneath
20 But the Lion just can't trust his teeth.

John Ciardi

Stopping Places

The long car journeys to the sea
must have their breaks, not always
in towns where there's no room
to park but at the pavement's edge,
5 in villages, or by the woods, or in lay-bys
vibrating to the passage of fast cars.
The seat's pushed forward, the boot's lifted,
the greaseproof paper
rustles encouragingly. The children
10 climb to the ground and posture about,
talk, clamber on gates, eat noisily.
They're herded back, the journey
continues.
      What do you think
15 they'll remember most of that holiday?
the beach? the stately home?
the hot kerb of the promenade?
No. It will often be those nameless places
where they stopped, perhaps for no more
20 than minutes. The rank grass
and the dingy robin by the overflowing
bin for waste, the gravel ridged by
numerous wheels and the briared wood
that no one else had bothered
25 to explore, the long inviting field
down which there wasn't time
to go — these will stick in their memories
when beauty spots evaporate.
Was it worth the expense?
30   but
these are the rewards of travelling.
There must be an end in sight
for the transient stopping places
to be necessary, to be memorable.

Molly Holden

The Song of the Whale

Heaving mountain in the sea,
Whale, I heard you
Grieving.

Great whale, crying for your life,
5 Crying for your kind, I knew
How we would use
Your dying:

Lipstick for our painted faces,
Polish for our shoes.

10 Tumbling mountain in the sea,
Whale, I heard you
Calling.

Bird-high notes, keening, soaring:
At their edge a tiny drum
15 Like a heartbeat.

We would make you
Dumb.

In the forest of the sea,
Whale, I heard you
20 Singing,

Singing to your kind.
We'll never let you be.
Instead of life we choose

Lipstick for our painted faces
25 *Polish for our shoes.*

Kit Wright

156

The Blind Men and the Elephant

It was six men of Indostan,
  To learning much inclined,
Who went to see the Elephant
  (Though all of them were blind),
5 That each by observation
  Might satisfy his mind.

The First approached the Elephant,
  And, happening to fall
Against his broad and sturdy side,
10 At once began to bawl,
'God bless me! but the Elephant
  Is very like a wall!'

The Second, feeling of the tusk,
Cried — 'Ho! what have we here
15 So very round and smooth, and sharp?
  To me 'tis mighty clear
This wonder of an Elephant
  Is very like a spear!'

The Third approached the animal
20 And happening to take
The squirming trunk within his hands,
  Thus boldly up and spake:
'I see' — quoth he — 'the Elephant
  Is very like a snake!'

25 The Fourth reached out his eager hand
  And felt about the knee:
'What most this wonderous beast is like
  Is mighty plain' — quoth he —
''Tis clear enough the Elephant
30 Is very like a tree!'

The Fifth, who chanced to touch the ear,
  Said — 'E'en the blindest man
Can tell what this resembles most;
  Defy the fact who can,
35 This marvel of an Elephant
  Is very like a fan!'

The Sixth no sooner had begun
  About the beast to grope,
Than, seizing on the swinging tail
40 That fell within his scope,
'I see' — quoth he — 'the Elephant
  Is very like a rope!'

And so these men of Indostan
  Disputed loud and long,
45 Each in his own opinion
  Exceeding stiff and strong,
Though each was partly in the right,
  And all were in the wrong!

John G Saxe

The Smell of Cooking

The smell of cooking rising to my room
Speaks clear of childhood and of many things.
Always, these days, I'm near to tears because
My parents and myself are leaving home.
5 Even to things that hurt affection clings.

Day after day, I've sorted out my books:
Nothing sensational and yet the whole
Experience is like an open nerve.
My parents and myself exchange cold looks.
10 Oh, every room is like a brimming bowl

Where flowers are leaning out and wanting air.
We too. The smell of cooking rises high
But hardly touches me because I know
Three-quarters of me is no longer here.

15 And yet I love this torn, reproachful sky
And am afraid of where I have to go.

Elizabeth Jennings

If Once You Have Slept on an Island

If once you have slept on an island
    You'll never be quite the same;
You may look as you looked the day before
    And go by the same old name,
5 You may bustle about in street and shop;
    You may sit at home and sew,
But you'll see blue water and wheeling gulls
    Wherever your feet may go.
You may chat with the neighbours of this and that
10   And close to your fire keep,
But you'll hear ship whistle and lighthouse bell
    And tides beat through your sleep.
Oh, you won't know why, and you can't say how
    Such change upon you came,
15 But — once you have slept on an island
    You'll never be quite the same!

Rachel Field

Descriptions

Jamaican Bus Ride

The live fowl squatting on the grapefruit and bananas
in the basket of the copper-coloured lady
is gloomy but resigned.
The four very large baskets on the floor
5 are in everybody's way,
as the conductor points out
loudly, often, but in vain.

Two quadroon dandies are disputing
who is standing on whose feet.

10 When we stop,
a boy vanishes through the door marked ENTRANCE;
but those entering through the door marked EXIT
are greatly hindered by the fact that when we started
there were twenty standing,
15 and another ten have somehow inserted themselves
into invisible crannies
between dark sweating body and body.

With an odour of petrol
both excessive and alarming

20 we hurtle hell-for-leather
    between crimson bougainvillea blossom
    and scarlet poinsettia
    and miraculously do not run over
    three goats, seven hens and a donkey
25 as we pray
    that the driver has not fortified himself
    at Daisy's Drinking Saloon
    with more than four rums:
    or by the gods of Jamaica
30 this day is our last!

                                    A S J Tessimond

1 Apart from the word 'Jamaican', what evidence is there that this poem does not refer to a British bus ride?
2 What does the bus conductor do about the baskets on the floor? What notice do the passengers take of him? Quote the words.
3 What does the word 'dandies' mean and what does it suggest about the men?
4 How do we know that the passengers do not get on and off the bus in an orderly manner?
5 Explain the passengers' fears about the bus driver.

6 Pick out the words or phrases which:
  a suggest bright colours,
  b suggest smells,
  c show a strong contrast.
  Pick out the word (verb) which describes the way the bus is driven.
7 Describe in your own words:
  a a school bus on the journey home
  b the scene on a bus at a shopping centre on a very wet Saturday before Christmas
  c the return journey on a coach trip either to the seaside or to a football match

Yorkshiremen in Pub Gardens

        As they sit there, happily drinking,
    their strokes, cancers and so forth are not in their minds.
        Indeed, what earthly good would thinking
    about the future (which is Death) do? Each summer finds
5   beer in their hands in big pint glasses.
        And so their leisure passes.

        Perhaps the older ones allow some inkling
    into their thoughts. Being hauled, as a kid, upstairs to bed
        screaming for a teddy or a tinkling
10   musical box, against their will. Each Joe or Fred
        wants longer with the life and lasses.
        And so their time passes.

        Second childhood; and 'Come in, number 80!'
    shouts inexorably the man in charge of the boating pool.
15   When you're called you must go, matey,
    so don't complain, keep it all calm and cool,
        there's masses of time yet, masses, masses . . .
        And so their life passes.

                                    Gavin Ewart

159

Frost on the Shortest Day

A heavy frost last night,
The longest night of the year,
Makes the land at first light
Look spruced up for death,
5   Incurably white.

But the earth moving fast
Tips the shadow across
The field. It rolls past
Sheep who hold their ground
10 And into the hedge at last.

Not far behind, a track
Of frost is following
That the sun cannot lick
Completely green in time,
15 Before night rolls back.

Patricia Beer

November the Fifth

And you, big rocket,
  I watch how madly you fly
  Into the smoky sky
  With flaming tail;
5   Hear your thin wail.

Catherine wheel,
  I see how fiercely you spin
  Round and round on your pin;
  How I admire
10 Your circle of fire.

Roman candle,
  I watch how prettily you spark
  Stars in the autumn dark
  Falling like rain
15 To shoot up again.

And you, old guy,
  I see how sadly you blaze on
  Till every scrap is gone;
  Burnt into ashes
20 Your skeleton crashes.

And so,
  The happy ending of the fun,
  Fireworks over, bonfire done;
  Must wait a year now to remember
25 Another fifth of November.

Leonard Clark

My Sister Betty

My sister Betty said,
'I'm going to be a famous actress.'
Last year she was going to be a missionary.
'Famous actresses always look unhappy but beautiful,'
5 She said pulling her mouth sideways
And making her eyes turn upwards
So they were mostly white.
'Do I look unhappy but beautiful?'
'I want to go to bed and read,' I said.
10 'Famous actresses suffer and have hysterics,' she said.
'I've been practising my hysterics.'
She began going very red and screaming
So that it hurt my ears.
She hit herself on the head with her fists
15 And rolled off my bed onto the lino.
I stood by the wardrobe where it was safer.
She got up saying, 'Thank you, thank you,'
And bowed to the four corners of my bedroom.
'Would you like an encore of hysterics?' she asked.
20 'No,' I said from inside the wardrobe.
There was fluff all over her vest.
'If you don't clap enthusiastically,' she said,
'I'll put your light out when you're reading.'
While I clapped a bit
25 She bowed and shouted, 'More, more.'
My mother shouted upstairs,
'Go to bed and stop teasing, Betty.'
'The best thing about being a famous actress,' Betty said,
'Is that you die a lot.'
30 She fell to the floor with a crash
And lay there for an hour and a half
With her eyes staring at the ceiling.
She only went away when I said,
'You really look like a famous actress.'

35 When I got into bed and started reading
She came and switched off my light.
It's not much fun
Having a famous actress for a sister.

Gareth Owen

A few more difficult

The Merry Go Round

Under the roof and the roof's shadow turns
this train of painted horses for a while
in this bright land that lingers
before it perishes. In what brave style
5   they prance — though some pull wagons.
And there burns
a wicked lion red with anger . . .
and now and then a big white elephant.

Even a stag runs here, as in the wood,
10   save that he bears a saddle where, upright,
a little girl in blue sits, buckled tight.

And on the lion whitely rides a young
boy who clings with little sweaty hands,
the while the lion shows his teeth and tongue.

15   And now and then a big white elephant.

And on the horses swiftly going by
are shining girls who have outgrown this play;
in the middle of the flight they let their eyes
glance here and there and near and far away —

20   and now and then a big white elephant.

And all this hurries toward the end, so fast,
whirling futilely, evermore the same.
A flash of red, of green, of gray, goes past,
and then a little scarce-begun profile.
25   And oftentimes a blissful dazzling smile
vanishes in this blind and breathless game.

Rainer Maria Rilke

At first this poem seems to be a description of the children and figures on a merry-go-round, but if you look carefully at the way the poet describes the scene you will see, or at least feel, that it suggests deeper thoughts to him. Read it two or three times carefully, note the description, then answer the questions.

Lines 1–8

1 What does 'this bright land' (line 3) refer to?

2 Which word suggests that the horses are magnificent and which words tell us that even on the unreal world of a merry-go-round they are restricted.

3 Look at the words 'lingers/before it perishes' (lines 3 and 4).
a What does it refer to in the description of the actual scene of the fairground?
b Could it refer to anything about life in general?
c Do you now think that 'this bright land' could have another meaning?

Lines 9–15

4 Which words show that the young boy is probably afraid?

5 What do you think he is afraid of?

6 Why does the poet repeat the line 'And now and then a big white elephant'?

Lines 16–20

7 In what way are the girls different from the children described in the earlier part of the poem?

8 Why do you think their eyes are looking elsewhere?

Lines 21–26

9 Which words describe how fast the merry-go-round is moving?

10 When things move they go from one point to another. Does this apply to the movement on the merry-go-round? Give two or three lines of explanation.

11 After considering your answer to the previous question, what do you think lines 21 and 22 mean?

In general

12 The poet obviously likes colourful scenes. Pick out the variety of colours in this description.

13 Pick out any parts where you think the movement of the lines (i.e. rhythm) matches well what the poet is describing in them.

14 The animals on a merry-go-round are not meant to look like real animals. Pick out the words or phrases which indicate this.

15 Describe in a similar way and as vividly as you can:
a a waxworks museum
b a go on the Big Dipper or Corkscrew
c the Haunted House or Hall of Mirrors at a funfair

The Meadow Mouse

I

In a shoe-box stuffed in an old nylon stocking
Sleeps the baby mouse I found in the meadow,
Where he trembled and shook beneath a stick
Till I caught him up by the tail and brought him in,
5   Cradled in my hand,
A little quaker, the whole body of him trembling,
His absurd whiskers sticking out like a cartoon-mouse,
His feet like small leaves,
Little lizard-feet,
10   Whitish and spread wide when he tried to struggle away,
Wriggling like a minuscule puppy.

Now he's eaten his three kinds of cheese and drunk from his
    bottle-cap watering-trough —
So much he just lies in one corner,
15   His tail curled under him, his belly big
As his head; his bat-like ears
Twitching, tilting towards the least sound.

Do I imagine he no longer trembles
When I come close to him?
20   He seems no longer to tremble.

II

But this morning the shoe-box house on the back porch is empty.
Where has he gone, my meadow mouse,
My thumb of a child that nuzzled in my palm? —
To run under the hawk's wing,
25   Under the eye of the great owl watching from the elm-tree,
To live by courtesy of the shrike, the snake, the tom-cat.

I think of the nestling fallen into the deep grass,
The turtle gasping in the dusty rubble of the highway,
The paralytic stunned in the tub, and the water rising —
30   All things innocent, hapless, forsaken.

Theodore Roethke

Once upon a Time

Once upon a time, son,
they used to laugh with their hearts
and laugh with their eyes;
but now they only laugh with their teeth,
5   while their ice-block-cold eyes
search behind my shadow.

There was a time indeed
they used to shake hands with their hearts;
but that's gone, son.
10 Now they shake hands without hearts
while their left hands search
my empty pockets.

'Feel at home,' 'Come again,'
they say, and when I come
15 again and feel
at home, once, twice,
there will be no thrice —
for then I find doors shut on me.

So I have learned many things, son.
20 I have learned to wear many faces
like dresses — homeface,
officeface, streetface, hostface, cock-
tailface, with all their conforming smiles
like a fixed portrait smile.

25 And I have learned too
to laugh with only my teeth
and shake hands without my heart.
I have also learned to say, 'Good-bye,'
when I mean 'Goodriddance';
30 to say 'Glad to meet you,'
without being glad; and to say 'It's been
nice talking to you,' after being bored.

But believe me, son.
I want to be what I used to be
35 when I was like you. I want
to unlearn all these muting things.
Most of all, I want to relearn
how to laugh, for my laugh in the mirror
shows only my teeth like a snake's bare fangs!

40 So show me, son,
how to laugh; show me how
I used to laugh and smile
once upon a time when I was like you.

Gabriel Okara

The language we use

The language we use

Every word we use has a job to do.

Sometimes it can do the job on its own:

'Hey'   'Who?'   'You'   'Me?'
'Yes'

At other times it needs to join with other words to form PHRASES and SENTENCES.

The jobs words do on their own are called *Parts of Speech* and the two main types are NOUNS and VERBS. Along with nouns go pronouns, adjectives, prepositions and with verbs go adverbs.

The first main type of word is the NOUN

Nouns are names of things. 'Things' here includes living things, people, animals, places, feelings, qualities, as well as objects.

A

If it is a *name* it is a NOUN. If it is a NOUN then it is the name of something.	boy, girl, car, football, Jean, Smith, happiness, London, dog, chair, width, tree

A(i)   *COMMON NOUNS* are the names of types or categories. Unless they are at the beginning of a sentence they do not start with a capital letter, e.g. school, boy, girl.

A(ii)   Names of individual people, places or things are called *PROPER NOUNS* and in English they always start with a capital letter, e.g. Tiddles, Lesley, London, Europe, Blackpool Tower, Brighton Pier.

Exercises

In the first two following sentences capital letters have been left out. Rewrite the sentence with the capital letters correctly placed. In the other sentences insert the appropriate proper nouns.

1 in the films about tarzan, his son is called boy and his wife jane.

2 when we won the cup at wembley we beat manchester united.

3 I live near to . . . . which is a small town in . . . .

4 The children, ... and . . . ., have a dog called . . . . and a hamster called . . . .

5 In spite of her name Mrs . . . . does not live in a . . . . However Mr . . . . does make clothes.

6 My favourite football team is . . . . Their nick-name is . . . . and they play at . . . .

A(iii)   Names of qualities, e.g., happiness, sadness and most words ending in *'ness'*. *Note* the spelling change:

happy — happi<u>n</u>ess
high — h<u>e</u>ight

Exercises

Give the name of the quality which comes from the first word given.

lovely	— loveliness
wide	— width
deep	
lonely	
warm	
broad	
slim	

167

A(iv) Names of groups of individuals are called *COLLECTIVE NOUNS*, e.g. team, orchestra. There is often confusion whether to regard these as single nouns or plural nouns, e.g.

The team *is* playing away.
The orchestra *are* out of tune.

The general rule is: if you are thinking of the group as a unit use singular, but if you are thinking of them as a group of individuals use plural. Do not mix the singular and the plural:

The team *are* playing *their* second game this week.

Exercises

Fill in the missing blanks with the appropriate words.
1 United . . . . playing without . . . . best forward.
2 When our netball team . . . . playing at home, most of the school watches . . . .
3 The jury . . . . divided in . . . . opinion.
4 A flock of birds . . . . seen on the lawn, but as soon as the cat saw . . . ., ... flew away.

B

> A PRONOUN is a word we use to avoid repeating a noun, e.g. John was speaking to Jean.
> *He* was speaking to Jean.

If it replaces a person's name it is called a *PERSONAL PRONOUN*, e.g. he, she.

The main thing to remember about personal pronouns is that they change according to the job they do in the sentence, e.g.

He was talking to her, but *she* was not listening to *him*.

If the pronoun is the subject of the verb, that is if it is carrying out the action, then the forms to use are:

I, we, he, she, they.

If the pronoun is the object of the verb, that is receiving the action of the verb, or if the pronoun comes after a preposition (see page 170), then the forms to use are:

me, us, him, her, them.

e.g. Between you and *me*
For you and *me*
You and *I* went to school together
I was speaking to him, *he* was speaking to *me*

Exercises

Change the underlined nouns in the following sentences to personal pronouns.
1 The soldiers were marching away.
2 Ian was looking for Ben when Jane came in.
3 The boys arrived before the girls.
4 Jane told Betty that Mary had gone away.

NOTE how the use of the personal pronouns in the last sentence can cause confusion.

C

> ADJECTIVES are words which tell us more about the noun or pronoun, generally by describing them or pointing them out.

The *tall* boy
The *intelligent* girl
That man
Seven hours
A *red* balloon

Exercises

Supply suitable adjectives for the following:
1 On the morning of the . . . . . . day after Christmas, I was very . . . . . . because I received . . . . more . . . . presents.
2 Although the weather was . . . . and . . . . I was still not too . . . . as I knew it would improve.

C(i) When we compare one noun with another we often use a special form of adjective, e.g.

A lion is fast, but a cheetah is faster.

We have added 'er' to the word fast to show a comparison. This form is known as the *COMPARATIVE* and is used for comparisons between two items. If the adjective is long, instead of adding 'er' we use the word 'more' e.g.

beautiful, more beautiful

Note the spelling changes in the following:

fat	fatter
fit	fitter
lonely	lonelier
happy	happier

C(ii) If we take the comparison one stage further we get what is known as the *SUPERLATIVE* form, e.g.

fit, fitter, fittest

The superlative is formed by adding '*est*' to the end of an adjective, or if the adjective is long by using the word 'most', e.g.

beautiful, most beautiful

Strictly speaking if only two items are being compared then the comparative should be used. However, we frequently say 'The best team lost' when referring to a game between two teams.

NOTE
a *Position of Adjectives* Normally they come before the noun, but they may come after, particularly after forms of the verb *to be*; e.g.

The night is dark
The rain was heavy
He was afraid

b *Few* and *fewest* refer to number, *less* and *least* refer to amount; e.g.

Fewer than four people attended, less than half accepted.

Exercises

1 Write out the comparative and superlative forms of:

great dry good small happy
much thin bad old little
interesting

2 Write out sentences containing the following correctly used:

the better team   the best team   the best man   fewer   less than

D

A PREPOSITION is a word which is normally placed before a noun or pronoun and shows the relationship between the noun and another word in the sentence.	by, which, from, in, into, on, end, for, above, between, among

NOTE The preposition should be followed by the object form of the personal pronoun (see **B**).

e.g.   for you and *me*
     between you and *me*
     to *him*
     from *me*

Exercises

Pick out the prepositions in the following sentences:
1 I went into the room, spoke to Bill and then left.
2 We do not go to school on Saturdays.
3 They were standing near the door next to my room.
4 Divide the cake into four parts with this knife.

The second main type of word is the VERB

E

| A VERB is a word which tells us what a noun (or pronoun) *does* or *is*. | He *runs* away
The plane *crashed*
He *seems* happy
She *is* happy |
|---|---|

The form and spelling of the verb changes according to:
- whether the noun is in the singular or plural
- the time the action takes place, i.e. the tense of the verb

E(i) Singular and plural

he *is* — they *are*
the girl *speaks* — the girls *speak*
The word which carries out the action of the verb is the *subject*.
If the subject is in the singular the singular form of the verb is used.
If the subject is in the plural the plural form of the verb is used, e.g.

I *am*, but we *are*
She *was*, but they *were*

Sometimes when a plural word comes between the subject and the verb it leads us to use the verb in the plural. Strictly speaking this is wrong, but certainly in spoken English it nearly always happens, e.g.

A *large number* of boys were running across the road.

Exercises

Pick out the correct form of the verb in the following:
1 You and I is/are in the team.
2 John and Jean is/are related to me.
3 The team was/were well beaten.
4 A woman, with two children, is/are waiting in the surgery.
5 A woman and two children is/are waiting in the surgery.
6 Neither Bill nor Jean was/were present.
7 Everyone of us is/are invited.
8 We was/were robbed.
9 A number of us are/is going.

E(ii) Tenses

Actions take place in time, either the *past*, the *present* or the *future*.
We use different forms of the verb to show the time of the action, e.g.

Past	Present	Future
I was	I am	I shall/will be
I was speaking	I speak/I am speaking	I shall speak/I shall be speaking

a The *present* tense gives little difficulty, but note that we sometimes use it in a story even though the actions took place in the past, e.g.

Well this girl comes up to me, looks me straight in the face, and tells me I'm a liar.

b The *future* also gives little difficulty except the difference between 'shall' and 'will'.

If the *simple future* is meant then 'shall' is used when 'I' or 'we' is the subject, e.g.

I shall go   we shall leave

'Will' is used for other subjects, e.g.

you will go   they will be leaving

If you want to express *determination* as well as the future then this order is reversed, e.g.

I/we will go   = determination
he/they shall go   = determination

However this is falling out of use especially in speech when we can emphasise the words we want.

c The *past* tense is more complicated as there are many different forms of it, e.g.

I was speaking   I spoke   I have spoken

The important thing to note is that for some verbs there are different forms and spelling for the past tense on its own (I *spoke*) and the past tense using 'have' (I have *spoken*). These should not be confused.

Exercises

Find out and learn the correct forms of the past tenses for the following:

Present	Simple Past	Past with 'have'
I speak	I spoke	I have spoken
They go	They went	They have gone
He writes		
We do		
She sings		
They come		
I ring		
You wake		
She breaks		
I light		
He says		
They pay		

Note

a Some verbs ending in 'd' or 't' do not change for either type of past tense, e.g.

I hit   I hit   I have hit

Other verbs like this are:

cut, let, put, shut, split, spread, bet

b Some verbs ending in a consonant and 'd' change the 'd' to 't' in the past tenses, e.g.

I ben*d*   I ben*t*   I have ben*t*

Other verbs like this are:

build, lend, send, spend

c Some verbs with an 'ee' sound ending in 'd' change the 'ee' to single 'e' in the past tense, e.g.

I bleed   I bled   I have bled

and also '*lead*' (when pronounced 'leed'), e.g.

I lead, I led, I have led

d The form of the verbs used with '*have*' is also the form we use with the verb *to be*, e.g.

I have *broken* the cup
The cup is *broken*

e This form of the verb (known as the past participle) can also be used as an adjective, e.g. a broken cup

171

F

Just as adjectives tell us more about nouns, so **ADVERBS** describe or tell us more about verbs.

I am talking *quietly*, listening *secretly*, while you are waiting *there*.

Exercises

Write down *three* adverbs that go well with the following verbs:
e.g. *to drive slowly, dangerously, recklessly*

to talk   to play the piano   to run
to fight   to wait   to think

F(i) Forms of adverbs

Many are formed by adding 'ly' to an adjective, e.g.

slow — slowly
quick — quickly
dangerous — dangerously

NOTE the spelling in such words as:

happy, happily   funny, funnily

There are some adverbs which are the same as adjectives, e.g.

fast (a fast runner — to run fast)
hard (a hard worker — to work hard)

F(ii)

An adverb may also be used to tell us more about an adjective or about another adverb, e.g.

a *newly* painted room
a *very* tall man
to run *more* quickly

F(iii) Comparison

Just as adjectives can be used to compare one thing with another, so adverbs may be used to compare one action of a verb with another. The comparative is formed by adding 'er' or using 'more', e.g.

faster   more dangerously

Likewise the superlative is formed by adding 'est' or using 'most', e.g.

fastest   most dangerously

The rules for the use of these two forms are the same as those for the use of comparative and superlative adjectives.

The other two parts of speech are CONJUNCTIONS and EXCLAMATIONS

G

A **CONJUNCTION** is a word which joins single words or groups of words.

'and' is the most common conjunction. Others include: but, when, after, before, if, although, because, as, since

Although conjunctions are only small words, they often control the meaning of a statement, e.g.

Although/As he plays for United he is a good player.

How does the use of either of these conjunctions change the meaning?

H

> An
> EXCLAMATION
> (or interjection)
> is a word which
> interrupts a
> sentence. It may
> also be an
> exclamation at the
> start of
> the sentence.

yes, no, indeed,
hello, goodbye, good
morning, ha! ha!

Exclamation marks may be used with these words.

I Groups of words

These may be *PHRASES*, *CLAUSES* or *SENTENCES*.

I(i) Phrases

> A PHRASE is a
> group of words
> which does not
> contain a verb and
> subject.

in the room
after the party
out of the sky
before 9 o'clock

Exercises

Use the above phrases and the following to form full sentences. Remember, use capital letters at the start of the sentence.

> listening to a new album
> out of the rain
> in the dark
> walking down the street
> on the top floor
> with a few friends

Phrases should go as close as possible to the words they are connected with, e.g.

> *In the middle of the road* I saw an injured dog.
> I saw an injured dog in the middle of the road.
> He was mowing the lawn *with a new machine*.
> He was mowing the lawn with his little brother.

How does the position of the phrase in each of the above sentences affect the meaning?

I(ii) Clauses

> A CLAUSE is a group of words containing a verb and subject. It may make full sense on its own or other words may need to be added in order for it to make full sense.

after the game was over
when all the dogs barked
who is the best player
where we are going

Exercises

The following are clauses which need other words in order to complete the meaning. Make full sentences out of them. Clauses need not come at the beginning of the sentence, but do not forget a capital letter for the first word of the sentence.

as I went out
after the bus had gone
before school started
whenever it snowed
if you switch the TV on
as you are so clever
although John was ill
who was the first to arrive

I(iii) Sentences

> A SENTENCE is a group of words containing a subject and a verb and it makes sense on its own. It starts with a capital letter and ends with a full stop.

I was very happy there.
The weather was pleasant.

Exercises

Divide the following into sentences using full stops and capital letters:

the day started pleasantly enough with bright sunshine it looked as though it was going to be a lovely sunny day for the games half way through the morning clouds started to form and by lunchtime there were signs of rain at 1.30 p.m. the first drops fell by 2.00 p.m. it was raining heavily sports day had to be cancelled.

General exercises

1 List the nouns, adjectives, verbs and adverbs in the above passage.
2 There is at least one error in each of the following sentences. Write out the corrected sentences.

a them boys done it
b crossing the road a bus ran into him
c was you there when it happened
d between you and I the best team lost
e she works at the houses of parliament
f when the orchestra was ready they started to play
g some people say england when they should say great britain
h before the disco started the lights fused
i he knocked the shed down with a friend
j a large number of people were present
k I sent them boys running away

Index

Acknowledgements

We are grateful to the following for permission to reproduce copyright material:

Associated Book Publishers (UK) Ltd for extracts from pp 44–5, 59, 65–6, 80, 136 *The Secret Diary of Adrian Mole Aged 13¾* by S Townsend (pub Methuen, London); B T Batsford Ltd for the poem 'School Report' by C Paine from p 119 *Children's Book of Comic Verse* ed C Logue; The British and Foreign Bible Society for an extract from the *Good News Bible* (c) American Bible Society 1976 (pub Bible Societies/Collins); Blandford Press Ltd for an extract from pp 84–5 *Modern Stories for School Assembly* by N Cook; The Bodley Head and Viking Penguin Inc for an extract from pp 5–7 *The Cartoonist* by B Byars Copyright (c) 1978 by B Byars; the author's agents for 'The Gift' from *The Day it Rained Forever* by R Bradbury (pub Hart-Davis MacGibbon Ltd); Jonathan Cape Ltd for the short story 'His First Flight' from *The Short Stories of Liam O'Flaherty*; the author's agents for the poems 'What Has Happened to Lulu?' and 'Who?' from pp 15, 96 *Figgie Hobbin* by C Causley (pub Macmillan); Chappell & Co Inc, EMI Publishing Ltd and International Music Publications, J Albert & Son for the poem 'The Lion and Albert' by M Edgar (c) 1933 Francis Day & Hunter Ltd., London. Copyright renewed, all rights in USA & Canada controlled by Chappell & Co Inc International copyright secured. All rights reserved; the author's agents for an extract from 'Murder in School' from *Golden Rain* by D Clark; Wm Collins Sons & Co Ltd for the poem 'The Fate of the Supermarket Manager' from *Rabbiting On* by K Wright; the author's agents for extracts from the short stories 'The Landlady' from *Kiss Kiss* by R Dahl (pub Penguin) and 'The Umbrella Man' from *More Tales of the Unexpected* by R Dahl (pub Michael Joseph); the author, L Davies for an extract from 'In the Fashion' from BBC Radio *Speak*; André Deutsch for the poem 'Horrible Things' from *Seen Grandpa Lately?* by R Fuller and an abridged extract from *The Wide Sargasso Sea* by J Rhys; Dobson Books Ltd for the poem 'November the Fifth' from *Collected Poems and Verses for Children*' by L Clark; Faber and Faber Ltd for 'The Song of the Jellicles' from *Old Possum's Book of Practical Cats* by T S Eliot and 'The North Ship: Legend' from *The North Ship* by P Larkin; Faber and Faber Ltd and Doubleday & Co Inc for the poem 'The Meadow Mouse' from *The Collected Poems of Theodore Roethke* (c) 1963 by Beatrice Roethke as Administratix of the estate of Theodore Roethke; Victor Gollancz Ltd for the poem 'Yorkshiremen in Pub Gardens' from *No Fool Like an Old Fool* by G Ewart; Harper & Row Publishers Inc for the poem 'Why Nobody Pets the Lion at the Zoo' from *The Reason for the Pelican* by J Ciardi (J B Lippincott Company) Copyright (c) 1959 by J Ciardi; William Heinemann Ltd for extracts from the play 'Noah' by A Obey trans by A Wilment and the poem 'Jamaican Bus Ride' by A S J Tessimond from *Seven Themes in Modern Verse* ed M Wollman (pub Harrap); William Heinemann Ltd and Doubleday & Co Inc for the poem 'If Once You Have Slept on an Island' from *Taxis and Toadstools* by R Field Copyright 1926 by Century Company; A W Holden for the poem 'Stopping Places' by M Holden from *The Honest Ulsterman* ed F Ormsby Copyright A Holden; the author's agents for the poem 'The Smell of Cooking' by E Jennings from p 61 *Seven Themes in Modern Verse* ed M Wollman; Michael Joseph Ltd for the extract entitled 'Hilde Coppi to Her Mother' from pp 203–4 *Between Ourselves* ed K Payne; Longman Group Ltd for the short story 'The Boy Judge' from *Tales from the Arabian Nights* ed J Turvey (Longman NMSR Series); Thomas Nelson and Sons Ltd for an abridged extract from 'A Real Good Smile' from *The Goalkeeper's Revenge and Other Stories* by B Naughton; New Directions Publishing Corporation for the poem 'Roast Swan Song' trans by G F Whicher in *The Goliard Poets* Copyright 1949 by G F Whicher; Octopus Books Ltd for the recipe 'Coffee Granita' from *Just Desserts* (pub Octopus Books Ltd); the author, G Owen for the poem 'My Sister Betty' from *Song of the City* by G Owen and J Hills (Fontana); Oxford University Press for the poem 'A Close Encounter' by A Rumble from *Upright Downfall: poems by Barbara Giles, Roy Fuller and Adrian Rumble* (c) A Rumble 1983; Pan Books Ltd for 'The Good Samaritan' from *A Child's Bible* re-written by S Steen (pub Pan Books); Penguin Books Ltd for the poem 'The Song of the Whale' from p 17 *Hot Dog and Other Poems* by K Wright (Kestrel Books 1981) Text Copyright (c) 1981 by K Wright; The Post Office for an extract from the pamphlet *Writing a Letter* (c) The Post Office; Resources for Learning Ltd for slightly adapted extracts from an article by H Pickles pp 4–5 *Payday* May 1982 and an article by M Shepherd pp 3, 12 *Payday* May 1983 (c) Payday, National Girobank's Schools Magazine; the author, N F Simpson for his poem 'One of Our St Bernard Dogs is Missing'; Stainer & Bell Ltd for an extract from the poem 'The Lord of the Dance' by S Carter (c) Stainer & Bell Ltd; Times Newspapers Ltd for an extract from the article 'Her First Pop Concert' by M Young from p 9 *The Times* (20/1/84); Understanding British Industry for an extract from pp 6/7 *Industry in the Countryside* CBI Education Foundation, distributed by Resources for Learning Ltd for Understanding British Industry; The University of California Press for the poem 'The Merry Go Round' by R M Rilke from *Rainer Maria Rilke: 50 Selected Poems* trans C F MacIntyre (c) 1940, 1968 by C F MacIntyre; Charles Vyse Associates for 'Clive's Story' from *Go Greek!* Charles Vyse 1983 Sunmed Brochure; the author's agents for an extract from *The Freedom Tree* by J Watson.

We have been unable to trace the copyright holders in the following material and would appreciate any information that would enable us to do so: the short story 'The Tiger in the Tunnel' by Ruskin Bond from *Modern Indian Short Stories* ed Suresh Kohli (Heinemann 1976); the poem 'Once Upon a Time' by Gabriel Okara from *Poems from Black Africa* ed Langston Hughes (Indiana University Press); the poem 'Frost on the Shortest Day' by Patricia Beer; the poem 'The Fringe on the Sea' by A L Hendriks from *Changing Islands* ed Boagey (pub UTP 1983).

Suit of Lights

Poems by Tom Cunliffe

*To Mandy,
with very best wishes.
love
Tom
X.*

Pighog Press
PO Box 145
Brighton BN1 6YU
England UK

info@pighog.co.uk

www.pighog.co.uk

Twitter www.twitter.com/pighog

Design by Curious
www.curiouslondon.com

Contents

inspection

in falling sleet
old wolves track birds–
feathers scatter

I take a pelt
off-white with hints of grey
dry fur in my hands

sliding the drawer shut
darkness covers *okami*
deep snow smothers him

okami - Japanese Wolf. Extinct c. 1905

tarpan

across her lawn
to a cave
and steps

torch beams
touch a stallion
running point to a herd

fingering their shapes
she follows the ceiling
of valleys

and plains
that run on
to the forests of Poland

stampeding off cliffs
she hears them leap
voiceless

Tarpan. European Wild Horse. Extinct c.1800

Hide

Hairs, once rufous
are now
a faded cinnamon,
a desert dune.

And hooves, so fleet
have gone walkabout –
      a pot of glue to stitch
      and bind a drum
      or fit a handle to a knife.

Each skin – chestnut to terracotta dark:
dark about the rump;
pale about the throat –
whose footsteps trample over breath
                   and pulse,
the freedom of a moving heart.

The female is unknown.

Rufous Gazelle. N. Africa. Extinct c.1930

Question?

There is a mute suspicion
as if, in a mirror
she is looking back,
the unquiet eye of dumb surveillance;
      a sentence of figures,
      a dark axle load of hay,
      a man with a stick
      Let it pass
and through them, a thread of light –
                     the trees.

A flash
but nothing boils;
a worn coin
newly bundled up
ship shape;
      a red zebra
      what is this
      unfinished
      a zebroid
      is it
      from where?

Even as they peeled her skin away
she still strode out
as though she were an Andalusian mare,
nostrils flared,
until her flesh fell like a closing ball.
Laid out flat
her stripes of cream and tan rang
as if October earth had been cut open,
each a rich brick and mortar seam.
The tanners brushed away their sweat,
stretching her out cured,
fit for a drawer,
ready to be rolled, itemised,
recorded on page,
now part of a treasury called *fewness*.

Quagga. S.Africa. Extinct 1884

The horn sack

An empty sky

                    the early stars

a blind spot, comma

                  a patina of myth.

Below, in leaves, they sail

               at each others pace

pass unspoken lands

               secrets wandering.

In swamp grass

                 each footfall

almost a whisper

               fills with moisture.

The bough's a porch

                 a gown of sorts

she pauses before

               a strand of pasture.


```
her  head  turns  to  the  right        fixed
have  I  been  here  before          listening
ears    and  flies            the  bolt  clicks
nostrils            wind                whistles
lead    fizzles          through  the  leaves
turns  her  dull  silver  back              flees
leaps      crashes          tongue-tied
```


              Another shot
                louder
                louder
                 louder
                 louder
                  aah

Unborn Alpha feels its way in Hamburg Zoo.
Along the Shiang they are grinding horn –
spoon handles bound for Sheffield.

Schomburgks Deer. Thailand. Extinct c. 1932

Enclosure

Between the glue and stitch
of this theatrical scene
something worms within
this storm-tossed chest.
Do you hear it,
an owls wing,
a cluster of late birds calling?
Try and coax this inattentive head,
that leaves us running low,
somewhere in that lonely space between
dried grasses and the cabinet frame –
our hands prone up against the pane.

All that remains of its broad rigidity –
something of a tiger, hyaena, wolf,
are these hoopoe stripes that crown the spine
to a tail still rising, eager as any whippet's.
So here he is, packed into a racing trap,
tapered in an enclosure of glass
where he has,
do you hear,
forgotten his lines,
besieged in dust.

Thylacine. Tasmania. Extinct 1934

Ewe

The track east of Caer Caradoc, beside the pines. Foxes entered it last night. There shouldn't be any smell just use your scarf. Leave the kids in the truck. Reverse up within 6 ft, unhook the wire and drop it down. You'll need to loop it under the shoulders so pull the head and negotiate it back on itself behind the front legs, until it comes up on all fours. It might snort but it's only gases. Don't rush or you'll pull it's head off. Slowly ease the motor in reverse until it hangs clear. I'm not sure what's underneath so take the plastic bags. Don't worry the birds will clear up. If a lamb follows give it to the kids to hold.

crows perch around the head
pecking her eyes
listening

You might think

         you might think   night bird like yap
piercing the canvas   a shock suddeness and   into dog silence
     coming across the field   from the veranda.....patio
it happened a long time ago   she sleeps on   the scrutiny of waiting
       I doze   sounds violate   moving across

     again from the foliage   silence is inaction   screams carry
   a frieze of trees   a dog fox calling his troop   a hollow piping
around her throat   a breaking yelp   stretched out   beneath the canvas
       cloth wiped air   the order of olive trees

tender border of cow parsley   and bramble   her legs open in dry leaves
    yellow squall   through fields and pools   chatter disrupted
the acoustic orchard   silent hives   following cries   sounds violate

days sleep   it happened a long time ago   a vixen coming around
   barks mutate   chorus   stroking her throat   the fox bickers
shaped and bolting loose   severance of voice   infant stoniness

Tableau

It's conceivable that the old woman lying in the road, shouldered across the traffic bollard, has it all, for three young angels with bare midriffs are in attendance. The shadow of a builder from the Xypex Roofing Co covers them he is crouched on one knee as though pulling the ceiling down to eye level. His van is murmuring further up the road, in conversation with its brother exchanging secrets; for there are many episodes to explain, including those about yellow curves and straight blues. For now, the woman can do little but wiggle her toes in their coffins and look up at the cluster of gulls peering back at the man who knocked her over. Her eyes circle his face, this, the man who reminds her of her own son who cannot be here for he is serving time for burglary with menace. Her thin bones are settling, heaving a sigh of relief, moving back into place but there is barely a leap in her stride and she still hasn't seen the blood. A heavy blanket covers her thin neck the way roofing felt, or tiles overlap – it makes sense. She is warm and cosy. They are measuring out the skid marks with flashing lights and lasers, measuring her body and how far the baby is away from her left arm. A dog handler talks quietly to his German shepherd, the road sweeper leans on his broom, cars cruise by slowly, on their way to a gathering of their own.

Lago

As you wait for the lights of the train
to pass along the shore,
pause in this tongue less town
that has turned its back
on its former glory.
Wander through the yellow colonnades,
wait for the quiet bells,
the barriers falling over the empty track.

With time on your hands, visit this night –
when you would normally stroll,
the Museum of White Walking Sticks or
the House of Colanders, Soup Ladles and Oars.
The Collection of Spectacles, Lists and Prescriptions awaits,
every item hanging in its allocated space,
each a human distance apart,
labelled, categorised,
forbidden.

For the blind are staggering,
lost near the station,
the infirm hobble on the crossing,
the platform restaurant is closed for the season,
the chemist switches off his green lights
just about now
and rushes home.
Pause,
watch the lights flickering across the lake –
listen to the frogs discussing
your admission fee.

This business

This business of floating, ears under water
cashmere over your face

I'm inspecting the *traje de lures* –
the garnet and greens fly off, relocate.

Mirrors chug by, their arcade lights flashing
a series of left jabs.

Smeared in honey and dust,
grease nipples, batteries rebound from my fingers,

shovels and spanners are nailed to the floor.
Someone is removing the chairs.

Around me tea makers, chopping boards, flip-lid bins,
fireworks – a gash in the fertile night.

Hams swing from the ceiling – Seville, Jaen, Salamanca
names of battles, regions for olives

as tripping over a bag full of phones
I feel that I have betrayed you.

And you, you pile up the cake stand,
carefully brush away the crumbs

understanding the art of putting things down quietly.

Father
from **'rest'**

Kiss her all night, all day long, take no rest. People will pass, burdened with suitcases, throw them some rope so they can bind their packages. Listen for the cold freezing their breath – infant splits and cracks – it will be icicles forming on the words of the women. Hold your tongue to the sun of her breast, blue veins, downy white skin. Nuzzle in, journey between her thighs, holiday in the inlets of her toes; taste the cherry of her neck, the cinnamon of her vulva, the mango of mouths open. Close her eyes with tiles, her nostrils with mortar, only stop when feathers sprout from her shoulders and your own lips turn golden
Outside they pass, their suitcases dragging them down. And yes, they will pause, perhaps peer in, but you will never hear their smiles. They do that later, when alone – very alone.

> they pass
> weightless as sleep –
> flying over regret

Mother
from *'rest'*

Mother regarded them as lies, partners in crime, part of my grubbiness. Scything them to the floor she pinched them up like filo pastries, dragged away my wet sleep, stained from the tears of my dreams. Hauling them down to the laundry she drowned their smiles before bleaching them out in the morning sun where, beating them, she forced all their evil into the light. You could hear their tiny screams. Later, spitting on the iron face, she scalded their soft backs returning them to my bed subdued where, gently smoothing them out virginal, she read out her litany of starched curses. Finally, closing the shutters, she pulled down the blinds, locking them into their darkness without so much as a mention of her son.

> dark hair
> tangled in white thorn-
> a flurry of sleet

My father lies
from 'rest'

I am looking down
into a small feathered room
that is stroked in pink and plush
with swathes of golden bombazine.
I'm suspended above the red satin sheet
on which my father lies landlocked
clutching my mothers hand.
They have been walking in the country
knee deep in white freesias
reliving the urgency of their wedding night
when the Milky Way came to their door.
She wears her air-hostess uniform with black silk stockings
and has just wiped his brow with good fortune.
They are surrounded by a collection of ivory and glass dildos,
tins of *Duchess of Nassau* perfumed talc, mint imperials
and photographs of their laughing child.
I am in the rafters, along with the cuckoo and the wrens,
keeping the outside sealed in and the white walls
                          of the corridors locked out.
Occasionally mother revives him
with her modern lipstick,
reminds him again of their little secret
when he played a naughty boy
and nurse had to be called so many times.
Again she says *Hold my plump thighs*
and do not consider escape.
Her fingers are pained in plasters
for she has treadled the rich velvets into sweeps
and bows and pinched and hooked father to where
he now rests, among the fluffy lilac cushions.
They lie far off, sated, smiling up at their son,
listening to the lamps hissing in the courtyard,
the trams beyond circling the house.

Listen

Stand me up
as if I were a table,
then scrub me down.

Cover me with bread crumbs,
crushed glass,
sinew and hair –
pin out my skin.

The voice in my body
continues –
is memory a searchlight?
Is a bandage a box?

My face is an envelope
protecting my soul,
cover it with coins.

You know what to do –
pick up the pieces.

A chair attempts suicide

You all dangle on hooks
but I have flown
my quills blazing,
my stubs falling differently each time.
My gestures were clean, outspoken,
I have flown.

A crash of limbs
and my nipples furnish the floor,
my ribs spilling among seed, can flips,
odd bits of plastic, broken grasses
and a hardy plant
worn to a corpse.
I am a basket of leaves.

Perhaps I am more awake
for I know this is not an embrace,
I see you illuminated by the dryness
                    of the moon.
Like a sprinkling of icing sugar
the frost has changed everything,
whitewashing the seats of the infirm.

I'm not telling lies.
In this body corset,
my back knuckled up,
I am forced to tell lies.
Put your ears to the hive
                    and listen.

Striding

She runs as if she's in love –
lightfoot,
as if she's crossing the street
to where her lover's arms await.
Dainty,
she jogs as if this journey
could go on and on
as her feet slow to a samba beat so
her breasts can rise up to his lips.

Splashing out
I watch her skirt the lawn,
cross the plaza, piazza,
take off along the promenade,
glide on to meet him –
her other lover,
her whiteness fading
all along the chain fence
into empty trees,
dark odours,
to open up her mouth and kiss him
with her half tongue.

3.58 pm

It was 9.15 precisely when she tied him to the door jamb, straight after sex and breakfast in bed of boiled eggs and brioche. Before leaving through the orchard she placed a light bulb in his mouth whispering one more thing into his ear.

Now, the sun warm on her mink trim, lambs wool top and fingering her crutch, she is about to have her fourteenth orgasm of the day. Sipping her latte, she has just had one of those mad, rare moments of doubt, did she flick the switch *on* or *off?* It doesn't matter, today is one of those days when she just can't stop herself.

11.42 pm

She waits, her breasts high in the laced-up leather dress he asks her to wear for the customers. She is watching him prise apart frozen gammon steaks with the wrong knife, waiting for him to slit his wrist. When he does she'll rush him to the hospital again, blood pouring onto the taxi floor, leave him looking at the nurses in their uniforms. She'll go back home, stroke his pillow, the same way he strokes her soft leather arse, then she'll stuff it into her satchel.

She scrapes bacon rind into the bin, he licks the lipstick off the mugs.

There is no rush, she has been dulling the knife blade, sharpening the point and she knows what time the last train departs. That night she will hang the leather dress in the chiller, lay her lace-up boots in the freezer, then slip into her trainers before jogging slowly to the station in that sparkly pink tee-shirt she wears, the one with *Music* written across her tits.

Footsteps

What of memory?... I have forgotten. A table without a top, yet you dance frivolous upon it, stretching as if on a beam, easing your long limbs, twisting and turning. It takes time you tell me. I place my glass in the corner pass you up a bruschetta... you balance like a toast rack, your thighs twitching in the broad leaves. We think of tables as mistakes. Are they?... I want to wrap my arms around this one, love it the way I love you but its soul is missing, falling among the trees... among the other souls lost in the rain. I've been hearing things... my hand on your breast but not under your bra. If this were my table I'd squeeze it up against the wall, upend it on one leg, breath in the sap, place you at its centre where you can pirouette, view your own movements in the dark.

At night this table searches for those souls loosened by the rain. I see you fall across it motionless, with all the silence of a Perugino. Four legs are not enough

Perugino: the master of Rapheal

Funny

There are many ways to enter a pool
but she, distrustful of her whiteness,
                              finds new ones.
She scribbles,
fearful of what her body can do to itself,
            a piste for a cleavage
            blemishes for breasts
            every limb a mistake,
even her dyed white hair the very mirror of error.
The profundity of pain,
            to cut a long story short
            she died daily.
            She dies every day.

She kept walking away – a quizzical walk,
inclined.
Sometimes he followed,
saw something in her scribbling.
Their eyes and angels were different.

Her poses have the feel of an accident;
            the tilt of her head,
            lying open mouthed or
            the way her pony tail bobs with each long stride.
            To cut a long story short –
                        until she smiles,
then her body arches like a violin,
hair falls like a scroll
and her breasts become the smudges
                              he rubs away.

freesias

approach the stairs carefully
one step at a time   think
do not skip   think of the flies
avoid the window   she will come out
do not carry items such as fruit   or kitchen utensils
nothing with labels   cross in single file
think of your brain as a pomegranate   chase the boys
never flick the dog with your towel   sit on the wall
objects are subversive   don't fuck
a sneeze is acceptable   avoid the sun
don't count your obsessions   teddy can't swim
you could spin   use your sister's sleeve
certain things are plausible   be sure you don't tremble
attempt one thing at a time   laugh behind your hand
never acknowledge your audience   spread more rumours
be careful with your hands   try counting to ten
busybodies are present   hold onto the snow
waking does not help   can you hold on?
sometimes you'll have time on your hands   buy a stick insect
fill in the forms fill in the forms   do not come down
danger is only a motorway away   imagine it is tomorrow
never tire of coping   sort one from the other
when the sky is full of gulls   make fires in the garden
keep your hands clean   consider how you'll leap
occasionally things quieten   buy a new set of keys
cows eat their cud four times   learn to keep secrets
all they do is weep   set a good example
there are things of which we are certain   learn to speak Zit
the dog is too old to acknowledge you   do a water-colour
if you loose your thread   make a collection
if in doubt   smell the freesias
should you forget your name   make a long list
I wish I could help   go to your room

The second fishing trip of spring

A table drifted by,
its surface thinly splashed in sky.
There could have been a full moon.

Dawn brought a green mist,
snow melt swirling
through the river core.

We found the same table three days later
on a sand bank,
standing among the wrecked computers.

I took a photograph,
a heron and the bottles bolt upright.
Next day the river rose.

The table drifted off covered in snow
trailing a cloth, some cakes,
a plastic pack of olives.

Clothes, the colours of October
hung in the trees,
a line shared with the clouds.

Debra joined some trekkers for a short trip.
Don't throw stones I warned.
They pulled over some logs, lit a fire.

Next day I found her
hanging in the limbs of a maple,
her face black as ebony.
A beaver was eating olives.

She called down,
started telling me the joke about lies and dreams
and the little green men from Louisville, Kentucky.
She has me hooked every time.

Tom Cunliffe comes from Ellesmere Port, Cheshire. A painter/printmaker he studied Fine Art at Brighton. He is a former Vice-Chairman of the Printmakers Council. His work has appeared in numerous publications including The New Writer, Blithe Spirit, Lynx, Stoney Thursday and Contemporary Haibun. In 2007 he co-edited the Poetry South Anthology. He lives in Hove.

Acknowledgements

With thanks to Anne Collins, Tim Beech, Judith Cair and Jan Campbell.

Acknowledgements are made to the editors of the following publications in which some of these poems have already appeared:

This Business   The Vers Open

Ewe   Contemporary Haibun Vol 9 (Red Moon Press) USA

You Might Think   Poetry South

Hide Stony Thursday Book, Ireland